Benjamin Franklin and Canada

Also from Westphalia Press
westphaliapress.org

Benjamin Franklin and Canada

by Hon. William Renwick Riddell,
LL.D., F.R.S.C

WESTPHALIA PRESS
An imprint of Policy Studies Organization

Westphalia Press
An imprint of Policy Studies Organization
1527 New Hampshire Ave., NW
Washington, D.C. 20036
info@ipsonet.org

ISBN-13: 978-1-63391-111-6
ISBN-10: 163391111X

Cover design by Taillefer Long at Illuminated Stories:
www.illuminatedstories.com

Daniel Gutierrez-Sandoval, Executive Director
PSO and Westphalia Press

Rahima Schwenkbeck, Director of Media and Marketing
PSO and Westphalia Press

Updated material and comments on this edition
can be found at the Westphalia Press website:
www.westphaliapress.org

BENJAMIN FRANKLIN AND CANADA.

BY THE HONOURABLE WILLIAM RENWICK RIDDELL,
LL.D., F.R.S.C.,
Justice of the Supreme Court of Ontario.

INTRODUCTION.

[Note: It having been suggested that it would increase the value and interest of the Paper read before the Historical Society of Pennsylvania on Benjamin Franklin's Mission to Canada and the Causes of its Failure, were some account given of his part in earlier years in having Canada become part of the British Empire, I have therefore here prefixed portion of an Address before the Empire Club of Canada at Toronto, November 15, 1923, dealing with this little known but very important episode in the life of Franklin and in the history of the world. The Empire Club very gladly gives its consent to the use of this Address by its sister organization, the Historical Society of Pennsylvania; and, sending its warmest greetings, hopes that the unity between and among the English-speaking peoples may continue and increase *in aeternum*.—W. R. R.]

The death blow to the old British Empire was struck in Canada in 1759, on the Plains of Abraham when Wolfe died victorious, cheered in death by the cry, "They run."

The blow, however, narrowly failed of being ineffective; it might well have produced no wound at all, not to speak of one that was fatal; and had it not been for Benjamin Franklin, the old British Empire might have

1

not received even a shock but have survived for many years.

Benjamin Franklin, printer, journalist, scientist, diplomatist, moralist, statesman, patriot, all in the first rank, was in 1757, at the age of fifty-one[1] sent to London by the Colony of Pennsylvania with a petition to the King, George II, that Pennsylvania might be permitted to tax the lands of the Penn estates for the defence of the Colony from the French and Indians. It was during his residence as Agent for Pennsylvania at the Court of St. James (Massachusetts and Connecticut also utilized his services) that the ancient Universities of St. Andrews and Oxford honoured themselves as well as him by conferring upon him the degrees of LL.D. and D.C.L. for his literary and scientific attainments: and to his friends and admirers, he was thereafter "the Doctor."

He was still in London when Quebec surrendered in September, 1759.

England was weary of war; the Seven Years' War which she had entered in 1756 to save Prussia from destruction by France and her allies—*absit omen*—glorious as it was, was depleting her resources; and, in 1759, it was not going too well with her ally, Frederick. The Government headed by Pitt were set on prosecuting the war with vigour and were fairly well supported by the country. The splendid victories on this Continent were encouraging but not sufficiently so to prevent voices in some influential—generally, indeed, Tory—circles being raised to stop the war and give up to France the conquered territory. Franklin opposed this step whenever and wherever an opportunity offered. We find him writing to Lord Kames from London, January 3, 1769, saying:—"No one can more sincerely rejoice than I do, on the reduction of Canada; and this not merely as I am a colonist but as I am a Briton. I have long been of opinion that the *founda-*

2

tions of the future grandeur and stability of the British Empire lie in America; and though like other foundations they are low and little now, they are, nevertheless, broad and strong enough to support the greatest political structure that human wisdom ever yet erected. I am, therefore, by no means for restoring Canada. If we keep it, all the country from the St. Lawrence to the Mississippi will in another century be filled with British people. Britain itself will become vastly more populous by the immense increase of its commerce; the Atlantic sea will be covered with your trading ships; and your naval power, thence continually increasing, will extend your influence round the whole globe and awe the world. If the French remain in Canada, they will continually harass our colonies by the Indians, and impede if not prevent their growth, your progress to greatness will at best be slow, and give room for many accidents that may forever prevent it.''[2]

But Franklin did not confine his efforts to private letter writing: he talked—and he was a most persuasive talker—to all of the slightest influence with whom he came in contact. The suggestion made by ''some among our great men'' who in 1759 had begun to prepare the minds of the people to surrender Canada because to keep it would draw on Britain the envy of other nations and occasion a confederation against her, that Canada was too large and not worth possessing anyway, he combated ''every day and every hour,'' and, as he rightly thought, with some success. He knew the English people, and he employed with skill and acumen the arguments which would have the greatest weight. The old British Empire was built on the plan of the old Roman Empire—Colonies and Provinces existed and were retained not for themselves but for the Mother Country. There was indeed no direct tribute exacted as in Roman times; but the Colonies paid an indirect tribute in affording a market for English goods and English trade—England was an essentially trading nation, and all her conquests had been for commercial advantages. The money spent for defending the Colonies was a premium of insurance against loss of trade. Accordingly, Franklin's weightiest argument was that by keeping Canada, the nation would save two or three millions a year, then spent in defending the American Colonies: and, moreover, the Colonies would thrive and increase much more rapidly and so furnish a vast additional increase in the demand for British goods.

He did not confine himself to such arguments as this, but indulged in many other topics which he urged on occasion according to the company he was in or the persons he addressed.

Franklin as a man loyal to his Province and his mission, had always in view in these discussions the interests of America; he did not trouble himself then or later about the interests of Canada, and only in a minor degree about the interests of the Mother Country.[3]

But Franklin had another arrow in his quiver, more effective still; and that he now sped with marvellous skill. He turned to account his dexterity and ability as a pamphleteer.

It was the age of pamphlets, and it is possible that there were some written by Franklin which have disappeared or cannot be identified as his; but two we know of with certainty. The first in point of importance, and probably in point of time is the celebrated ''Canada Pamphlet.''[4]

William Pulteney who had been a power in his day had destroyed his political prestige in 1742 by accepting a peerage, becoming Earl of Bath.[5] He was hated by the King, George II, and never again was of importance; although the King, in 1746, invited him to form a government, he failed.

But he was never content with his position: from

time to time he made public appearances like "an aged raven:" his speeches had a little of the old ring of the times when Walpole feared his tongue more than another man's sword. The Earl had selected as travelling tutor for his son, the Rev. John Douglas, a native of Fifeshire, a graduate of Oxford and a former Army chaplain: he presented the clergyman to two churches and they were close friends. Dr. Douglas (he took his D. D. degree in 1758) had undoubted ability, and at the Earl's direction he wrote several political pamphlets.[6]

Pulteney early in 1760 induced Dr. Douglas to write a pamphlet on the war: and Dr. Douglas accordingly wrote "A Letter to two Great men on the Prospect of Peace and on the Terms." The "two Great Men" were the elder Pitt and Newcastle who had formed a Coalition Government three years before and had raised and spent money for war purposes with a profusion which appalled more timid financiers—but which would in the recent war have been considered trifling. This pamphlet Walpole calls "very dull": it dealt with the terms necessary to be insisted upon in the negotiations for peace, and gave reasons for preferring Canada to the conquests of the West Indies—Guadeloupe had been taken in January, 1759. This pamphlet was answered by another, by William Burke, entitled "Remarks on 'A Letter to two Great Men,' '' which contained opposite opinions on this and other subjects.[7]

Now was Franklin's opportunity, and he took advantage of it in the "Canada Pamphlet,"[8] which was published anonymously in 1760: a second edition eliding certain matter irrelevant to the general purpose and amending the terminology in some respects,[9] appeared in 1761, published with Franklin's name as author and is printed in Franklin's Works.[10] This is really a reply to the "Answer" and only incidentally is the "Letter" considered.

Franklin begins by demanding security from* the

"barbarous tribes of savages that delight in war and take pride in murder, subjects properly neither of the French nor the English, but strongly attached to the former by the art and indefatigable industry of priests, similarity of superstitions and frequent family alliances. These are easily and have been continually instigated to fall upon and massacre our planters even in times of full peace between the two crowns, to the certain diminution of our people and the contraction of our settlements." He points out the absurdity of Forts as a sufficient protection against the French and the Indians: and urges that the possession of Canada is the only security. Answering the claim that the American colonists were wanting conquests made for them, he spiritedly says that these colonists "are in common with the other subjects of Great Britain anxious for the glory of her crown, the extent of her power and commerce, the welfare and future repose of the whole British people . . . they have been actuated by a truly British spirit to exert themselves beyond their strength." Then he artfully suggests that if Canada is retained, the people in the colonies will spread over the mountains and take up land making a market for English goods, whereas if not, they must for their own safety remain confined within the mountains, go into manufacturing and afford goods "cheap enough to prevent the importation of the same kind from abroad, and to bear the expense of its own exportation"—"But" he adds "no man who can have a piece of land of his own sufficient by his labour to subsist his family in plenty is poor enough to be a manufacturer and work for a master . . . while there is land enough in America for our people, there can never be manufacturers to any amount or value." Franklin counters: "how can the author of the Remarks counselling the return of Canada to France, justify the retention of Guadaloupe which he represents as of so much greater value?"

Then he goes into the relative value of the two countries in an argument eminently fitted for his audience.[11]

True, the trade with the West Indies is a valuable one but it has long been at a stand—limited as our sugar planters are by the scantiness of territory, they cannot increase much and that evil will be little helped by our keeping Guadaloupe: the trade with the people in the northern colonies doubles in about twenty-five years— the exports to Pennsylvania alone having increased in 28 years 17 times, the population having increased but four times. Suppose Guadaloupe does export £300,000 in sugar every year: who profits by it? Why, the French inhabitants of the Island who will not be dispossessed and who will spend no more than before on English manufactures. But Canada retained and so the American colonists made safe, "the annual increment alone of our present colonies without diminishing their numbers or requiring a man from hence is sufficient in ten years to fill Canada with double the number of English that it now has of French inhabitants"— and all will be customers of England.[12]

The most curious part of this pamphlet is that in which he contests the claim in the Answer that the American colonies would become dangerous to Great Britain if allowed to grow. "Of this, I own, I have not the least conception when I consider that we have already fourteen separate governments on the maritime coasts of the continent: and if we extend our settlements, shall probably have as many more behind them on the inland side. Those we now have are not only under different governors, but have different forms of government, different laws, different interests and some of them different religious persuasions and different manners. Their jealousy of each other is so great that, however necessary an union of the colonies has long been for their common defence and security against their enemies and how sensible soever each colony has been of that necessity, yet they have never been able to effect such an union among themselves, nor even to agree in requesting the mother country to establish it for them. Nothing but the immediate command of the crown has been able to produce even the imperfect union, but lately seen there, of the forces of some colonies.[13] If they could not agree to unite for their defence against the French and the Indians who are perpetually harassing their settlements, burning their villages and murdering their people, can it be reasonably supposed there is any danger of their uniting against their own nation which protects and encourages them, with which they have so many connections and ties of blood interest and affection and which it is well known, they all love more than they love each other? In short, there are so many causes that must operate to prevent it that I will venture to say, an union amongst them for such a purpose is not merely improbable, it is impossible.''

Franklin's task was not yet complete: the cry for peace continued and to meet that by casting discredit on its authors he wrote another article which he sent to the *London Chronicle;* it was afterwards published in the *Gentlemen's Magazine.* He pretended to have found in a bookstall an old quarto without title page or author's name, containing discourses, addressed to some King of Spain translated into English and said in the last leaf to be printed in London by Bonham Norton and John Bill, "Printers to the King's most excellent Majestie, MDCXXIX;''[14] he adds "The author appears to have been a Jesuit. . . . Give me leave to communicate to the public a chapter so *apropos* to our present situation (only changing Spain for France) that I think it well worth general attention and observation, as it discovers the arts of our enemies and may therefore help in some degree to put us on our guard against them.'' There had been writings and discourses he says in Britain like those recommended in the Spanish book; and although so far they had little effect as "all ranks and degrees among us persist hitherto in declaring for a vigorous prosecution of the war in preference to an unsafe, disadvantageous or dishonourable peace, yet as a little change of fortune may make such writings more attended to and give them greater weight, I think the publication of this piece as it shows the spring from whence these scribblers draw their poisoned waters, may be of public utility."

Then he copies what purports to be a chapter from the old book.

"Chap. XXXIV.

ON THE MEANES OF DISPOSING THE ENEMIE TO PEACE"

It is in the main a recommendation to the King of Spain who is supposed to be at war with England to gain by proper Meanes (i. e., bribery) "Menne of Learning (in England) ingenious Speakers and Writers who are nevertheless in lowe Estate and Pinched by Fortune . . . in their Sermons, Discourses, Writings, Poems and Songs to . . . magnifie the Blessings of Peace . . . expatiate on the Miseries of War, the Waste of Christian Blood, the growing Scarcitie of Labourers and Workmen, the Dearness of all foreign Wares and Merchandise, the Interruption of Commerce, the Capture of Ships, the Increase and great Burthen of Taxes. Let them represent the Advantages gained against us as trivial and little Import; the Places taken from us as of small Trade and Produce, inconvenient for Situation, unwholesome for Ayre and Climate, useless to their Nation and greatlie chargeable to keepe, draining the home Countrie both of Menne and Money. . . . " &c., &c.—precisely the arguments which had been used to bring on a peace with surrender of Canada, and precisely the arguments used by the agents of Germany in the late War. Nothing was better adapted to throw suspicion on the Pacifists, whom Franklin looked upon as dangerous to England, and more dangerous to America.[15]

Franklin's argument prevailed: Canada was retained: the fear of French Canadians and French Indians was removed: what Vergennes had prophesied took place: the Thirteen Colonies rebelled and the old British Empire was rent in twain to be in time destroyed and a new British Empire built on the old foundations, but of "practically independent sister States cooperating for the common good,"[16] whose Prime Ministers meet at the Imperial Conference, the Prime Minister of Great Britain "on terms of perfect equality with him and with each other."[17]

[The Paper continues with an account of Franklin's mission to Canada in 1776 and its failure, and concludes as follows:]

Franklin left Canada a very few days after he entered it, leaving it to work out its own destiny: and so far as is known, he never saw it again.

But Canada has him in great measure to thank for her being as she is the brightest jewel in the British Crown and for her flying the flag that braved a thousand years the battle and the breeze; and she may forgive him for the fruitless attempt to sever her destinies from the rest of the British world. He succeeded because he could persuade Englishmen, he failed because he could not persuade French-Canadians; for both his success and his failure, we are devoutly thankful at this time of Thanksgiving. His success made possible the destruction of the old British Empire—his failure made possible the creation of the new, better and greater British Empire.

WILLIAM RENWICK RIDDELL.

Osgoode Hall, November 12, 1923.

(Thanksgiving Day)

Benjamin Franklin and Canada.

REFERENCES.

[1] "The Americana," Vol. VIII, Art. "Franklin, Benjamin," makes him in the 41st year of his age when in 1757 he was sent to London by his Province; it also says that he spent the next 41 years of his life practically all in the diplomatic service. As Franklin was born in 1706 and died in 1790, these figures should be 51st and 31 respectively.

[2] *The Life of Benjamin Franklin written by Himself;* By John Bigelow; London, 1879, Vol. I, p. 399. This letter as it seems to me may well put an end to the supposition that Franklin had an *arrière pensée* in writing the "Canada Pamphlet" about to be spoken of in the text. See my Article "The Status of Canada," *Journal issued by American Bar Association*, June, 1921, pp. 293, sqq.

[3] See his letter to John Hughes from London, January 7, 1760; Bigelow, *op. cit.*, p. 402. He ends this letter: "And, on the whole, I flatter myself that my being here at this time may be of some service to the general interest of America." My own opinion is that his being there at that time revolutionized the world and changed the course of human history.

[4] The full title is "The Interest of Great Britain considered with regard to her Colonies, etc."—the pamphlet is very rare (my own copy cost me £8). It was almost certainly published by May, 1760; it is probably that referred to in Franklin's letter to Lord Kames dated London, May 9, 1760—Bigelow, *op. cit.*, Vol. 1, p. 404—in which he says "Enclosed you have the production such as it is."

[5] Horace Walpole, Earl of Orford, says in a letter to the Countess of Ossory from Strawberry Hill, July 17, 1792, that Pulteney "had gobbled the honour but perceived his error too late for on the day that he entered the House of Lords, he dashed his patent on the floor in a rage, and vowed he would never take it up; but it was too late—he had kissed the King's hand for it." Walpole's *Letters*, Cunningham's edition, Vol. IX, p. 379; see also do. do. Vol. I, p. 143. Walpole certainly got the better of him; and he himself said "he lost his head and was obliged to go out of town for three or four days to keep his senses." See D. N. B.,, Vol. XLVII, pp. 28, sqq.

[6] He should be remembered for his vigorous, able and successful defence of John Milton from the charge of plagiarism made against him by William Lauder, another Scotsman, and M. A. of Edinburgh. See D. N. B., Vol. XV, pp. 337, 338.

[7] Horace Walpole, Earl of Orford, says in a letter to George Montagu, from Arlington Street, January 14, 1760: "There is nothing new but a very dull pamphlet, written by Lord Bath and his chaplain Douglas, called a 'Letter to Two Great Men.' It is a plan for the peace and much adopted by the City, and much admired by those who are too humble to judge for themselves." Walpole's *Letters*, Cunningham's

edition, Vol. III, p. 278. Walpole does not seem to have mentioned the Answer or the Canada Pamphlet. I have not seen either the Letter or the Answer: the former I have seen advertised for sale only once and I failed to acquire it: I have never seen the latter advertised: the substance of them, however, is made sufficiently clear in the Canada Pamphlet. Bigelow does not notice them.

[8] It would seem that Franklin wrote this pamphlet on the request of Lord Kames. Writing to Kames from London, May 9, 1760, Franklin says: "I have endeavoured to comply with your request in writing something on the present situation of our affairs in America in order to give more correct notions of the British interest with regard to the colonies than those I found many sensible men possessed of. Enclosed you have the production such as it is. I wish it may, in any degree, be of service to the public." Bigelow, *op. cit.*, Vol. I, p. 404, thinks this the "Canada Pamphlet," and I agree with him.

[9] David Hume seems to have criticized the language of the pamphlet: Franklin in a letter to him from Coventry, September 27, 1760, thanks Hume for his "friendly admonition relating to some unusual words in the pamphlet. It will be of service to me." He admits *"pejorate"* and *"colonize"* are not in common use and gives them up as bad, "for certainly in writings intended for persuasion and general information, one cannot be too clear; and every expression in the least obscure is a fault." He thinks *"unshakeable"* clear but he gives "it up as rather low;" and "the word *inaccessible* though long in use among us is not as yet, I dare say, so universally understood by our people as the word *uncomeatable* would immediately be which we are not allowed to write." Bigelow, *op. cit.*, Vol. I, p. 412. "Pejorate," to make worse, is still an unusual and stilted word: Franklin in the first edition of the "Canada Pamphlet" in the "observations concerning the increase of mankind, &c.," omitted in the second edition used the word in the sentence "Slaves also pejorate the families that use them." *The Works of Benjamin Franklin, LL.D.*, 2d Ed., London, Vol. 2, p. 388. This essay was written in 1751. Robert Louis Stevenson uses the word (1893) in his *Catriona:* I do not recall its appearance elsewhere. It sounds odd to hear the word "colonize" characterized as obscure—it had been in use from Bacon's time, 1622; and is one of our commonest and most generally understood words; I do not know of a word to take its place. Franklin used it in the second edition, see p. 139. "Inaccessible" had been in use at least for two centuries and it is very common at the present time—"uncomeatable" is still taboo in literary circles but not unusual in familiar parlance.

[10] *The Works of Benjamin Franklin, ut suprâ*, Vol. 3, pp. 89–143— this edition being readily available, I shall cite it in this paper. It was "printed for Becket," London, 1761. Two editions of the "Canada Pamphlet" also appeared in Boston: and a long answer also was published. It seems quite certain that while Franklin supplied most of the information, Richard Jackson did most of the work on the "Canada Pamphlet," at least two-thirds of the text being his.

Benjamin Franklin and Canada.

[11] There never was a more astute diplomat than Franklin and he was extraordinarily able in feeling his audience and adapting his methods accordingly.

To indicate the strong feeling in favour of the retention of Guadeloupe it may be mentioned that Pitt in his Speech in the House of Commons, December 9, 1792, on the motion to approve the Preliminary Peace Treaty—he was so excessively ill that the House unanimously desired him to speak sitting—said that he had been blamed for consenting to give up Guadaloupe. . . . He wished to have kept the Island: he had been overruled on that point: he could not help it: he had been overruled many times on many occasions. He had acquiesced, he had submitted. . . . *The Parliamentary History of England* (Hansard), Vol. XV, col. 1264. The motion passed the House, 319 to 65, Pitt generally approving—he had left the Government with Temple shortly before on the question of War with Spain: the Papers relating to his negotiations with France are in do. do. cols. 1018–1210. The Peace was actually signed February 10, 1763.

[12] The expectation expressed concerning the French population of Canada is interesting. "Those who are Protestants among the French will probably choose to remain under the English government; many will choose to remove if they can be allowed to sell their lands, improvements and effects; the rest in that thin-settled country will in less than half-a-century from the crowds of English settling round and among them be blended and incorporated with our people both in language and in manners."

When Canada was retained on the Peace of 1763, it was confidently expected that it would soon be settled by an English-speaking community and not a few merchants came in to Quebec and Montreal from Britain and the American Colonies to the South; the Royal Proclamation of 1763 promised the protection of the English law; and free lands were offered to settlers. The expectation that many French Canadians would remove proved fallacious, as but a negligible part went to France, although they had full leave to dispose of their property and had eighteen months in which to do it. No great English-speaking immigration set in until the Revolutionary War; and the French refused to blend with the newcomers in language or in customs—rather the reverse was the case. The movement to unite the Canadas in 1822 was in essence a movement to overwhelm the French Canadians; and Lord Durham's scheme of Union (1840) had the same result in view. All these designs proved vain imaginings—the astute statesmen failed to reckon with the virility and love of their language of the French and the fertility of French mothers.

[13] In Pepperrell's expedition against Louisbourg, 1745, were troops from Massachusetts, Connecticut, Rhode Island and New Hampshire— Pennsylvania declined to join. Benjamin Franklin in Philadelphia wrote to his brother in Boston: "Fortified towns are hard nuts to crack, and your teeth are not accustomed to it; but some seem to think that forts are as easy to take as snuff"—and he used his influence against Pennsylvania joining.

13

Benjamin Franklin and Canada.

Parkman, A Half-Century of Conflict, Champlain Ed., Boston, 1897, Vol. 2, p. 70.

Probably the reference in the text is to the American contingent in the war then going on; troops were contributed by Massachusetts, Connecticut, Rhode Island, New Hampshire, New York, Pennsylvania, Virginia, Maryland, North and South Carolinas, New Jersey—not all at the same time or in the same expedition. "The Royal American Regiment" took part as an Imperial contingent in the campaigns of 1759, 1760.

[14] No doubt, Franklin had seen such a colophon: Bonham Norton (1565–1635) was a King's Printer: D. N. B., Vol. XLI, pp. 225, 226: but the book is a myth. The date of Franklin's production is not certainly known but Sparks says "its contents show it to have been written towards the close of the French war and probably in 1760 or the year following. Under the disguise of a pretended chapter from an old book and an imitation of an antiquated style he throws out hints suited to attract attention and afford amusement." I think Sparks quite underrates the purpose and effect of this communication: it is a most ingenious and telling document calculated to cast suspicion on the advocates of peace. The Ency. Brit. 11th Ed. Vol. II, p. 25, says it "had a great effect." I think, however, it is in error in dating it before the "Canada Pamphlet." See Bigelow op. cit., Vol. I, pp. 414, 415 and note. Franklin signed the communication to the London Chronicle, "A Briton."

While Franklin frequently declared that in the "Canada Pamphlet" he received considerable assistance from a learned friend who was not willing to be named but who is now known to have been Richard Jackson, Agent for Massachusetts and Connecticut, no one has ever doubted that Franklin was the sole and only author of this production.

[15] See this curious production in Bigelow, op. cit., Vol. I, pp. 416–420; the communication to the London Chronicle, do. do., pp. 414–416.

[16] The language of the Prince of Wales, as true as it is inspiring.

[17] The language of the Prime Minister of Great Britain, the Rt. Hon. Stanley Baldwin and of the former Prime Minister of Canada, the Rt. Hon. Sir Robert Borden.

BENJAMIN FRANKLIN'S MISSION TO CANADA AND THE CAUSES OF ITS FAILURE.

BY THE HONOURABLE WILLIAM RENWICK RIDDELL,
LL.D., F.R.S.C., &c.,
Justice of the Supreme Court of Ontario.

[*For References, see pages 142 to 158.*]

Benjamin Franklin was an accomplished diplomatist of great shrewdness and tenacity; and it was confidently expected by the Continental Congress that valuable results would follow from his mission to Canada in 1776.

His failure was pronounced: so far as we can now judge from extant documents, he was wholly unsuccessful—but it cannot fairly be said that any other result was possible in the existing state of affairs; his failure was due to circumstances over which he had, then at least, no control.

Tout comprendre c'est tout pardonner—or, if not quite that, tout comprendre ce rend très-indulgent.

It will be necessary to the understanding of Franklin's problem that we should examine the state of Canada at the time of his visit.

When de Vaudreuil in September, 1760, surrendered Montreal and, with it, Canada, to the British, General Sir Jeffrey Amherst by Article XXVII of the Capitulation agreed that: "The free exercise of the Catholic, Apostolic and Roman Religion, shall subsist entire."[1] The Definitive Treaty of Paris, February 10, 1763, whereby His Most Christian Majesty of France "cedes and guarantees to His Britannick Majesty, in full right, Canada with all its dependencies," contained in Article IV, the agreement of His Britannic Majesty "to grant the liberty of the Catholic religion to the inhabitants of Canada: he will, in consequence give the most precise and most effectual orders, that his new Roman Catholic subjects may profess the worship of their religion according to the rites of the Romish church as far as the laws of Great Britain permit."[2] At this time, it was believed by the Home Administration that the more northern of the Thirteen Colonies by reason of the increase of population had scarcely room for any more inhabitants,[3] and it was deemed wise to attract to Canada settlers, merchants and others, from the American Colonies as well as from the British Isles.

The Royal Proclamation of October 7, 1763,[4] recited that the King was "desirous that all Our loving Subjects as well of our Kingdom as of Our Colonies in America, may avail themselves with all convenient speed of the great benefits and advantages which must accrue therefrom to their Commerce, Manufactures and Navigation." The Proclamation stated that the King had erected four Separate Governments, Quebec, East Florida, West Florida and Grenada, with only the first of which, Quebec, we have any concern at this time.

It is important to bear in mind the Western and Southern boundaries of the new "Government" of Quebec; the Western boundary was a line (in the present Province of Ontario) running from the south end of Lake Nipissim (Nipissing) to the River St. Lawrence in 45 Degrees of North Latitude (about the present Town of Cornwall, Ontario). The southern boundary was along this parallel of latitude to Lake Champlain and "along the High Lands which divide the Rivers that empty themselves into the River St. Lawrence from those that fall into the Sea." The lands to the West, "lying about the Great Lakes and beyond the sources of the rivers which fall into the River St. Lawrence from the North," were intended "to be thrown into the Indian Country" for the fur-trade: while the limit to the south was so fixed as to prevent interference with the Colonies already established. The Lords of Trade in their representation to His Majesty, June 8, 1763, said: "The Advantage resulting from this restriction of the Colony of Canada will be that of preventing by proper and natural Boundaries, as well the Ancient French Inhabitants as others from removing and settling in remote places, where they neither could be so conveniently made amenable to the Jurisdiction of any Colony nor made subservient to the Interest of the Trade and Commerce of this Kingdom by an easy Communication with & Vicinity to the great River St. Lawrence. And this Division by the height of land to the South of the River St. Lawrence will . . . leave all your Majesty's new French Subjects under such Government as your Majesty shall think proper to continue to them in regard to the Right & Usages already secured or that may be granted to them." Moreover, the Lords of Trade urged that "Planting, perpetual Settlement and Cultivation ought to be encouraged" in Canada as in "Florida and the newly acquired Islands in the West Indies."[5] The Royal Proclamation says: "Whereas it will greatly contribute to the speedy settling our said new Governments that our loving subjects should be informed of our Paternal care for the security of the Liberties and Properties of those who are and shall become Inhabitants thereof, we have thought fit to publish and declare by this, Our Proclamation that we have in the Letters Patent under Our Great Seal of Great Britain by which the said Governments are constituted, given express Power and Direction to our Governors of our Said Colonies respectively, that so soon as the state and circumstances of the Said Colonies will admit thereof, they shall with the Advice and consent of the Members of our Council, summon and call General Assemblies within the said Governments respectively, in such Manner and Form as is used and directed in those Colonies and Provinces in America which are under Our immediate Government: and We have have also given Power to our said Governors with the consent of our Said Councils and the Representatives of the People so to be summoned as aforesaid, to make constitute and ordain Laws, Statutes and Ordinances for the Public Peace, Welfare and good Government of Our said Colonies and of the People and Inhabitants thereof as near as may be agreeable to the Laws of England and under such Regulations and Restrictions as are used in other Colonies: and in the meantime and until such Assemblies can be called as aforesaid, all Persons Inhabiting in or resorting to Our Said Colonies may confide in our Royal Protection for the Enjoyment of the Benefit of the Laws of our Realm of England." This, of course, was an express promise to all who were then or who were to be inhabitants of Quebec that they should have the protection of the laws of England until such time as they should have an Assembly representative of the people, to make laws for them—there was also what was almost an express promise that such a representative Assembly would be summoned by the Governor as soon as the circumstances of the Colony would allow.

General James Murray being appointed "Captain General and Governor in Chief in and over our Province of Quebec," his Commission, December 21, 1763, gave him the "power and authority with the advice and Consent of our Said Council . . . so soon as the Situation and circumstances of our said Province . . . will admit thereof and when & as often as need shall require, to summon and call General Assemblies of the Freeholders and Planters within your Government. . . ." "The persons thereupon duly elected by the Major Part of the Freeholders of the respective parishes or precincts and so returned," were to take the oath against the Pretender; and the Governor with his appointed Council and elected Assembly could make laws, statutes and ordinances—until an Assembly should be summoned, this power could be exercised by the Governor and his Council alone.[6]

Murray's Instructions[7] were to the same effect: they, however, were specific that he should conform with great exactness to the stipulations of the Treaty of Paris, February 10, 1763, as to the right of the Roman Catholic inhabitants to "profess the Worship of their religion according to the Rites of the Romish Church, so far as the Laws of Great Britain permit"; and that he was not to "admit of any Ecclesiastical Jurisdiction of the See of Rome or any other foreign Ecclesiastical Jurisdiction whatsoever in the Province."[8]

A number of immigrants from the British Isles and the North American Colonies settled in the Province of Quebec, many of whom claimed—some, no doubt, with justice—that they had been induced to do so by the promises in the Royal Proclamation: these new settlers were called "Old Subjects" while the French Canadians were called "New Subjects," the "Old Subjects" being generally Protestant, the "New Subjects" generally Roman Catholic.

When the country was still under Military Rule, *i.e.*, before the establishment of Civil Government pursuant to the Royal Proclamation, there was not much friction between these two elements—the French Canadian always expected until the very last that Canada would on the Peace be given back to France.[9]

But when Civil Government was introduced, it was not long before there was an agitation by some of the Old Subjects for an Assembly. The French Canadians cared nothing for such a body: while they enjoyed their religion and they were not interfered with in their customs, they were content—not so the Old Subjects.[10]

Benjamin Franklin's Mission to Canada.

Governor Murray formed a bad impression of the "Old Subjects" and he had a high opinion of the French Canadians—they were "perhaps the bravest and the best race upon the Globe," while the others were "Licentious Fanatics."[11] In 1766, there were 19 Protestant Families in the Parishes, the "other Protestants, a few half-pay officers excepted, are Traders, Mechanics and Publicans in Quebec and Montreal . . . the most miserable collection of men, I ever knew."[12]

There was another ground of dispute between the Old and the New Subjects—the latter desired the re-introduction of their former law[13] based as it was on the Coutume de Paris, and ultimately upon the Civil Law of Rome: the former insisted upon the Laws of England which, as we have seen, had been secured to them by the Proclamation of 1763. Ultimately the French Canadian prevailed, and the celebrated Quebec Act of 1774[14] was passed.

As this Act plays a very large part in subsequent events, it will be well to state its principal provisions so far as they bear upon our subject. In the first place, the former western boundary is removed: the Province of Quebec is to contain all the territory bounded by a line from Lake Champlain to the River St. Lawrence along the parallel of 45 degrees North Latitude then along the east bank of the River up to Lake Ontario, through Lake Ontario and the River Niagara, along the east and south east bank of Lake Erie to the western boundary of Pennsylvania, southward along this boundary to the River Ohio, along the bank of the Ohio to the Banks of the Mississippi and northward to the southern boundary of the Hudson's Bay Territory. We shall see that this extension of the Province was bitterly resented by the Colonies to the South, although it is expressly enacted "That nothing herein contained relative to the boundary of the Province of Quebec shall in any wise affect the Boundaries of any other Colony."[15]

Then is to be noted a provision which excited much indignation—more in the other North American Colonies than in Canada itself, be it said. Section 5 enacted that those professing the religion of the Church of Rome in the Province might "have hold and exercise the free exercise of the religion of the Church of Rome subject to the King's Supremacy, declared and established" by the Act of 1558, 1 Elizabeth, cap. 1—this was, of course, but implementing the promises of the Articles of Capitulation and the Definitive Treaty; and it is probable that this alone would not have so moved the Protestants to the South. But the same section provided "that the Clergy of the said Church may hold, receive and enjoy their accustomed dues and rights with respect to such persons only as shall profess the said religion"—this is the provision fulminated against as establishing the Roman Catholic Church.[16] Section 6 allows the King to make provision for the encouragement of the Protestant Religion and for the maintenance of a protestant Clergy out of the "rest of the said accustomed dues and rights"—and this was interpreted to mean the religion and Clergy of the Church of England.

The third feature in this Act strenuously objected to, both by the Old Subjects (or at least some of them) in Canada and the Thirteen Colonies, was the omission to provide for an Assembly, and the power given to the Governor and his nominated Council to legislate for the Province.[17] And the fourth, equally objected to, was the provision "that in all matters of controversy relative to property and civil rights, resort shall be had to the Laws of Canada as the rule for the decision of the same."[18] This last was a direct breach of an express promise of the King contained in the Royal Proclamation of 1763 as the preceding was of the implied promise. Nothing could excuse this breach of faith but the gravest necessity—this necessity, Sir Guy

Carleton, Lord Dorchester, the Governor, believed to exist and so did the Home Administration. *Sub judice lis est:* So far as my own investigations enable me to judge, I think they were right. The Act came into force, May 1, 1775—petition against, counter-petition for, it followed: and there was a very serious situation —many of the Old Subjects insisted on the rights of Englishmen, and some did not hesitate to say that they would have the rights of Englishmen even though that meant ceasing to be British.

Let us turn now to the south; the Quebec Act was assented to early in 1774:[19] Franklin was at the time in London and using all his influence against it—we find as early as July 23, 1774, a friend of his writing from London to Philadelphia "that detestable Quebec Bill which is so evidently intended as a bridle on the Northern Colonies."[20]

The celebrated Suffolk County (Pa.) Resolutions passed, September 6, 1774, were the first (so far as I can find) which publicly expressed the objection of the Colonists outside of Canada to the religious features of the Quebec Act. "10—That the late Act of Parliament for establishing the Roman Catholic Religion and the French laws in that extensive country, now called Canada, is dangerous in an extreme degree to the Protestant religion and to the civil rights and liberties of all Americans; and therefore, as men and Protestant Christians, we are indispensably obliged to take all proper measures for our security."[21]

It was not long before the Continental Congress spoke out—September 28, 1774, after condemning the Statutes, (1764), 4 George 3, c. 34; (1765), 5 George 3, c. 35; (1766), 6 George 3, c. 52; (1767), 7 George 3, cc. 41 and 46; (1768), 8 George 3, c. 22, as "subversive of American rights," Congress resolved, condemning "the Act passed in the same [last] session for establishing the Roman Catholic religion in the Province of Quebec,

abolishing the equitable system of English Law and
enabling a tyranny there to the great danger from so
total a dissimilarity of Religion, Law and Government
of the neighbouring British Colonies by the assistance
of whose blood and treasure, the said country was conquered from France.''[22] So far only the substitution
of Canadian law for the ''equitable system of English
Law,'' the omission to provide for an elective Assembly
and what was called the establishment of the Roman
Catholic Religion were all that could be found objec-
tionable in the Quebec Act.

But, Thursday, October 20, 1774, the Congress while
''avowing our allegiance to His Majesty,'' assailed the
''Act for extending the Province of Quebec so as to
border on the Western Frontiers of the Colonies, establishing an arbitrary government therein and dis-
couraging the settlement of British subjects in that
wide extended country: thus by the influence of civil
principles and ancient prejudicies to dispose the inhabitants to act with hostility against the free Protestant Colonies, whenever a wicked Ministry choose so to
direct them.''[23]

The address to the People of Great Britain, adopted
October 21, 1774, complained that ''by another Act, the
dominion of Canada is to be so extended, modelled
and governed as that by being disunited from us, detached from our interests by civil and religious prejudices, that by their numbers daily swelling with
Catholic Emigrants from Europe and by their devo-
tion to Administration so friendly to their religion,
they may become formidable to us and on occasion be
fit instruments in the hands of power to reduce the
ancient free Protestant Colonies to the same state of
slavery with themselves. . . . Nor can we suppress
our astonishment that a British Parliament should ever
consent to establish in that country a Religion that has
deluged your Island in blood and dispersed impiety,

bigotry, persecution, murder and rebellion through every part of the world."[24] (Only reverence for the Fathers will enable us to repress a smile at the rebuke by those themselves soon to become rebels, to the Church for "dispersing rebellion;" and perhaps the less said about "bigotry," the better.)

On the same day, Thomas Cushing, of Massachusetts, Richard Henry Lee, of Virginia, and John Dickinson, of Pennsylvania, were appointed a Committee to draft an address to the People of Quebec and Letters to the Colonies of St. John's (now Prince Edward Island) Nova Scotia, Georgia, East and West Florida "who have not deputies to represent them in this Congress."

Now, apparently for the first time, it seems to have struck these ardent protestants that after all, Roman Catholics have or at least might claim that they have some rights, that even French Canadians have the right to the laws and form of government which they prefer.

The address produced by the Committee—John Dickinson[25] is credited with its authorship—is as extraordinary a document as is to be found anywhere—whatever may be said of its candour, no "Philadelphia lawyer" ever showed more ingenuity in ignoring awkward facts.

It begins with a compliment to the Canadians who "after a gallant and glorious resistance" had, to the joy of the other Colonies, been "incorporated . . . with the body of English subjects . . . a truly valuable addition both on our own and your account expecting as courage and generosity are naturally united, our brave enemies would become our hearty friends and that the Divine Being would bless . . . you . . . by securing to you and your latest posterity the inestimable advantages of a free English constitution of government. . . . These hopes were confirmed by the King's Proclamation . . . in the year 1763, plighting the public faith for your full enjoyment of these advantages.'' But ministry had withheld these irrevocable rights—and ''as you, educated under another form of government, have artfully been kept from discovering the unspeakable worth of that form, you are now undoubtedly entitled to, we esteem it our duty . . . to explain to you some of its most important branches.'' No word of the undoubted fact that the Ministry was more than willing to grant that form of government and the Canadians would have none of it.

Then follows a philosophical discussion of the beauties of Representative Government with quotations from Beccaria and Montesquieu, of trial by jury (the French Canadian never got over his wonder that the English conqueror preferred to have his rights determined by the tailor and shoemaker rather than the judge), Habeas Corpus, ''holding lands by the tenure of easy rents'' (the Frenchman preferred his own ways of holding lands), freedom of the press (there was just one paper in the Province, the *Quebec Gazette,* first issued, June 21, 1764, and which could not live without government patronage).

The Quebec Act did not give them liberty of conscience in their religion—God gave it to them; nor the French laws—the Governor and Council could change them. Apparently the dangerous religion and law were not really advanced by the Act—but what becomes, then, of the grievance?

The Address goes on: ''We are too well acquainted with the liberality of sentiment distinguishing your nation to imagine that difference of religion will prejudice you against a hearty amity with us.

''You know that the transcendent nature of freedom elevates those who unite in the cause above all such low-minded infirmities. The Swiss Cantons furnish a memorable proof of this truth. Their union is composed of Catholic and Protestant states, living in the utmost concord and peace with one another and thereby

enabled ever since they bravely vindicated their freedom, to defy and defeat every tyrant that has invaded
them. . . . We do not ask you, by this address, to com-
mence hostilities against the government of our common sovereign . . . submit it to your consideration
. . . to meet together . . . and elect deputies who
. . . may choose delegates to represent your Province
in the continental congress . . . at Philadelphia on the
tenth day of May, 1775.

"In this present congress . . . it has been with . . .
. . . an unanimous vote, resolved that we should consider the violation of your rights by the act for altering
the government of your province as a violation of our
own. . . . "

This was adopted, October 26, 1774, and it was "Resolved that the address to the People of Canada be
signed by the President, and the Delegates of the Province of Philadelphia superintend the translating, printing, publishing and dispersing it. And it is recommended by the Congress to the Delegates of New
Hampshire, Massachusetts Bay and New York to assist
in and forward the dispersion of the said address."[26]

On the same day, October 26, 1774, the Congress
adopted an address to the King in which a complaint
was made, *inter alia,* against the Act, "for extending
the limits of Quebec, abolishing the English and restoring the French laws, whereby great numbers of English
freemen are subjected to the latter and establishing an
absolute government and the Roman Catholick religion
throughout those vast regions that border on the west-
erly and northerly boundaries of the free Protestant
English Settlements."[27]

There was an active correspondence between certain
discontented Canadians—almost all of them English-
speaking and in Montreal—and some of the leaders in
the Continental Congress: and somewhat exaggerated
accounts of the actually existing discontent with the

Quebec Act in Canada were sent from time to time to Philadelphia and elsewhere in the Thirteen Colonies. The City of Quebec itself was generally quiet; but there were several meetings of the dissatisfied at Montreal— the chief grievance being the power by the Act given to the priests to collect tithes. It is true that this was only to affect Roman Catholics, and, generally speaking, French Canadians, but it legalized the status of the priest, restoring to him rights which he had in the French period and under the Règne Militaire which lasted from the Conquest till after the Treaty of Paris. No little of the agitation was due to the influence of the Colonies to the South.

The Pennsylvania Delegates had the Address to the Inhabitants of Quebec, translated and printed by Fleury Mesplet, a Frenchman, then a printer in Phila-delphia: but before the French translation reached Quebec, one copy if not more, of the English text was sent there to some of the discontented. A translation into French was there made, and manuscript copies were circulated from hand to hand among the French— the only printer in the Province, who published the *Quebec Gazette,* refused to print it.[28]

This did not escape the notice of Sir Guy Carleton, the Governor, nor did a further attempt a few weeks later to bring the Address before the French—we find Carleton writing from Quebec, March 13, 1775, to Lord Dartmouth: ''Several of His Majesty's natural born subjects continue suggesting into the minds of the Canadians, an abhorrence of the form of Government intended by the Act of last Session and least they should not sufficiently understand the Letter addressed to them by the Continental Congress at Philadelphia, have been at the Pains to translate, and not succeeding with the Press here, have put themselves to the expense of sending it to some of the factious Printers to the Southward to be printed off: two or three hundred copies have actually been imported into the Province and I hope will prove of as little consequence as their former effort: it is needless to trouble your Lordship with a copy of this Letter as it has been transcribed I believe into every American Paper except the *Quebec Gazette.*''[29]

In addition to the written and printed appeals, there were those made *viva voce*—Carleton receives information from Montreal (of date, April 3, 1775): "There are some People lately come into this Province from New England who I suspect are no better than they should be. One is gone to Quebec and, as I am informed, a second is at Three Rivers and a third remains here ⌊i.e. at Montreal⌋. I am told that there are three more at La Prairie''; and a meeting had been held there on Saturday, for no good purpose.[30] Another report to Carleton from Montreal of April 6, 1775,[31] referring to these New Englanders, proceeds: "The Day before yesterday, most of the merchants as well as most of the English, Scotch and Irish of this Town, assembled at the Coffee House here and were harangued by the New Englander. I am told that their assembly was to chuse two Deputies to send to the Congress to be held at Philadelphia on the 10th of next May.'' The next day, April 7, the report is: "One New Englander, Brown, an Attorney and a member of the Provincial Congress at Cambridge, at a meeting of merchants held at the Coffee House, Tuesday last . . . read a letter addressed to Thomas Walker, Isaac Todd, Blake, Price, Haywood and to all friends of Liberty signed by Adams, Mackay and Warren,'' saying that the late Acts of Parliament were oppressive and unconstitutional—then Walker, a great Republican, harangued the meeting and moved a Committee of Observation like that at Cambridge and to send two Delegates to the Continental Congress. He received no backing. Todd would have nothing to do with the letter: Walker, Blake, Price and Haywood intend to answer the letter—"Brown is endeavouring to intimidate the Canadians by assuring them that if a man of them should dare to take up arms and act against the Bostonians,[32] 30,000 of them will immediately march into Canada "and lay waste the whole Country."

Thomas Walker was a well known personage of Montreal who had some years before had trouble with the military in which he came off second best: he does not seem to have received fair play—however that may have been, he was discontented with the Government and a constant source of trouble. He was in correspondence with Benedict Arnold, then at Crown Point, and kept him informed of affairs in Montreal. We find Arnold writing him from Ticonderoga, May 20, and from Crown Point, May 24, 1755, the latter[33] letter shows the kind of threat used against the Canadians.

"I beg the favour of you to advise me of the number of Troops with you . . . their movements and designs if possible and if joined by any Canadians or Indians. If any number of the former, you may assure them they will soon see our Army of Prinkins[34] here, men in the Heart of their Country."

The Battle of Bunker Hill was fought, June 17, 1775; the British soldiers on Bunker Hill were appealed to by the American Soldiers on Prospect Hill in a printed Address urging them not to imbrue their "Hands in the Blood of your Fellow-Subjects in America," as they were called upon to do because the American fellow-subjects would "not admit to be Slaves and are alarmed at the Establishment of Popery and Arbitrary Power in One Half of their Country"; and it was hoped that the British Soldiers would "not stain the Laurels you have gained from France by dipping them in Civil Blood."

It is probably too much to say that after the passage of the Quebec Act, it was the main object of attack and the chief reason for the Declaration of Independence: but it cannot be denied that anti-Catholic feeling had something to do with it—certainly this was manifested again and again.

All this was well known in Canada—a part of the 400 Old Subjects shared the sentiments of the revolutionaries: but hardly a handful of the 80,000 French Canadians could be won over.

The French Canadian while generally willing to defend his own country against invasion was nevertheless unwilling to join the British forces: Maseres writing to Lord Shelburne (afterwards Marquis of Lansdowne) from the Inner Temple, London, August 24, 1775, says that an Englishman arrived from Quebec brought the news that the "Canadians persist in refusing to act offensively against the other Americans but say they are ready to defend their own Province against any invasions the Americans shall attempt to make into it."[35] Carleton's efforts to form an effective Canadian force were without avail: and indeed, it was a somewhat general sentiment amongst Englishmen that such a scheme would be inadvisable in any event. Maseres' letter sufficiently explains this view: "I should be very sorry to see the Canadians engaged in this quarrel for two reasons: 1st, because I believe it would soon produce the ruin of their country, and 2nd, because if the event was to be otherwise and they were to subdue the other Americans, I should not like to see a Popish Army flushed with the conquest of the protestant and English provinces."[36]

Carleton went so far as to request Bishop Briand of Quebec to issue an Episcopal mandate to compel Canadians to enlist but the the Bishop declined, as it would be quite unsuitable for the occasion—he said that if the Governor wished, he would write a Circular Letter to all the priests in the country to direct them to use their best endeavors in the way of private con-

versation to induce the Canadians to engage their services. Carleton accepted the offer; the Bishop did so
write but the letter had no effect.[37]

Some of the Seigneurs endeavored to bring into force
their authority under the French law, to compel the
"habitants" to form a military corps: but the habitants
refused and mobbed their former officers, so that they
were fain to flee for safety.

The state of Canada in 1775 was perilous—there
were only a few troops to protect her, many of the English speaking population, perhaps the larger number
of them, were in sympathy with the American Colonists, while the French Canadians as a whole were determined not to act aggresively; and it was at least doubt-
ful whether they could be relied upon even to defend
Canada.

Carleton and Britain had in Bishop Briand, a tower
of strength: indeed, some Catholic writers do not hesitate to say that Bishop Briand saved Canada for
Britain.[38]   The last French Bishop, Pontbriand, dying
in June, 1760, Briand was consecrated in 1766 and he
steadily and strongly supported the loyalist cause.

He knew how his Church was looked upon in the
Thirteen Colonies—before 1776, Catholics were allowed
by law freedom of worship in two Colonies only, Maryland and Pennsylvania: and even in these Colonies,
they were denied the franchise: he knew the language
and sentiments of the Addresses of the Continental
Congress to the People of England in which his
religion was characterized as bloody and as spreading
"impiety, bigotry, persecution, murder and rebellion
through every part of the world:" he knew what value
to place upon the plausible statements of the Address
to the Inhabitants of Quebec—he thought that what
looked like a change of heart as to his Church was
transitory and deceptive—he felt that French Canadian Catholics had nothing to gain from association

with Colonies now rapidly approaching their independence—his Clergy were kept informed and, almost to a man, they remained loyal.

The Continental Congress were unnecessarily alarmed when, Thursday, May 18, 1775, the Resolution was passed with the Preamble: "Whereas there is indubitable evidence that a design is formed by the British Ministry of making a civil invasion from the Province of Quebec upon these Colonies for the purpose of destroying our lives and liberties and some steps have actually been taken to carry the said design into execution:" New York and Albany were recommended to remove Cannon and Stores from Ticonderoga; and Jay, Samuel Adams and Deane were appointed a Committee to prepare and bring in a Letter to the People of Canada.[39] Monday, May 29, the Letter To the Oppressed Inhabitants of Canada is approved—since the conclusion of the war, they were fellow-subjects and now fellow-sufferers, "devoted by the cruel edicts of a despotic Administration to common ruin"; "it was the fate of Protestant and Catholick Colonies to be strongly linked together," and they were invited "to join with us in resolving to be free and in rejecting with disdain the fetters of Slavery however artfully polished": they were told: "By the introduction of your present form of government or rather present form of tyranny, you and your wives and children are made slaves."[39] The fact that they had never had any other form of government and did not want any other form is not so much as hinted at.

When Arnold received orders to invade Canada by way of the Kennebec,[40] General George Washington wrote an Address to the Inhabitants of Canada: "To cooperate with this design and to frustrate those cruel and perfidious schemes which would deluge our frontiers with the blood of women and children, I have detached Colonel Arnold into your Country" [a sort of homoeopathy]. ''Necessaries and accommodations of every kind which you may furnish, he will thankfully receive and render the full value. . . . The United Colonies know no distinction but such as slavery, corruption and arbitrary domination may create.'' In his Orders to Arnold, he specifically directed him to ''check by every motive of duty and fear of punishment, every attempt to plunder or insult any of the inhabitants of Canada,'' even the death penalty to be inflicted.[41] There is no reason to suppose that Arnold did not do his best—but tradition relates, a century and a half thereafter, stories of robbery, insult and worse—Arnold had little ''hard money'' and had to pay in Continental Scrip (''not worth a Continental'') and his soldiers sometimes got out of hand.[42]

Montreal was taken by Montgomery in November, 1775, and left in charge of Wooster while Montgomery went to Quebec to join Arnold. Montgomery died and Arnold failed through the vigilance and skill of Carleton.

Montreal remaining in the possession of the Colonies, the Continental Congress, January 24, 1776, directed a Letter to be sent to the Inhabitants of Canada: ''We will never abandon you to the unrelenting fury of your and our enemies; two Batallions have already received orders to march to Canada.''[43] But another step was to be taken: on Thursday, February 17, 1776, it was ''Resolved, That a Committee of Three (two of whom to be Members of Congress) be appointed to proceed to Canada there to pursue such instructions as shall be given by Congress.''

The Members being chosen, that is, Doctor Benjamin Franklin, Mr. Samuel Chase, of Maryland, and Mr. Charles Carroll, of Carrollton, the Congress

''Resolved That Mr. Carroll be requested to prevail on Mr. John Carroll to accompany the Committee to

Canada to assist them in such matters as they shall think useful.

"Resolved That this Congress will make provision to defray any expense which may attend this measure"— a very prudent Resolution was added: "Resolved That eight tons of Powder be immediately sent to Canada for the use of the Forces there." A few days thereafter, Monday, February 26, 1776, a further reinforcement was agreed on: "Resolved That Monsieur Mesplet, Printer, be engaged to go to Canada and there set up his Press and carry on the Printing business: and the Congress engage to defray the expense of transporting him and his family and printing utensils to Canada and will moreover pay him the sum of Two hundred Dollars."[44]

It is now time to say a word or two of Doctor Benjamin Franklin in connection with the Quebec Act.

In the wonderful letter to his son written when returning to America on board the *Pennsylvania* Packet, Captain Osborne, bound for Philadelphia, dated March 22, 1775, Franklin speaks of a conversation at a meeting, February 5, 1774, with David Barclay and Dr. Fothergill[45] concerning the terms upon which a durable union might probably be produced between Britain and the American Colonies. He had written down "Hints" as to the terms, No. 11 of which was: "11. The late Massachusetts and Quebeck Acts to be repealed and a free government granted to Canada." Franklin notes that at the meeting of February 5, "11. The eleventh refused absolutely except as to the Boston Port Bill which would be repealed and the Quebeck Act might be so far amended as to reduce that Province to its ancient limits"

Then on February 16, Barclay submitted his counter suggestion.

"5. The several Provinces who may think themselves aggrieved by the Quebeck Bill to petition in their legislative capacities: and it is to be understood that so far as the limits of Quebeck beyond its ancient limits is to be repealed''[46]

Franklin arrived at Philadelphia, May 5, 1775, and was the next day, *nemine contradicente,* added to the Pennsylvania Deputies to attend the Continental Congress, May 10 [47]; and July 3, he was made President of the Committee of Safety at Philadelphia and directed to procure a model of a pike.[48]

It would serve no useful purpose here to review the course of Franklin after his return from England— let us proceed with the story of the mission to Canada.

While the Congress had determined upon a mission to Canada, there was no little difference of opinion as to the Instructions to be given the Commissioners: but at length, the Draft Instructions were considered, March 11, 12 and 19, and the Instructions were settled March 20, 1776. The most important of these was: that the Commissioners should represent to the Canadians, ''that the arms of the United Colonies having been carried into that Province for the purpose of frustrating the designs of the British Court against our common liberties, we expect not only to defeat the hostile machinations of Governor Carlton[49] against us but that we shall put it into the power of our Canadian brethren to pursue such measures for securing their own freedom and happiness as a generous love of liberty and sound policy shall dictate to them.'' Moreover, the Canadians were to be solemnly guaranteed in the name of Congress ''the free and undisturbed exercise of their religion'' and the priests ''the full perfect and peaceable possession and enjoyment of all their estates.''[50]

On March 23, the Commissioners or any two of them were given power to raise a number of independent Companies not exceeding six and to appoint officers; and $1066 2/3 in Continental money was given them in

addition to the $1000 in specie already paid to them—
the further sum to defray their expenses.[51]

The Commissioners made their way to New York,
thence, April 2, on a river sloop up to Albany where
they met General Schuyler; after a short delay they
went on to Ticonderoga and Montreal, arriving there,
April 29. They found the Army stricken with small-
pox and Arnold troubled with the sanitary and financial
situation. May 1, 1776, The Commissioners report to
Congress: "It is impossible to give you a just idea of
the lowness of the Continental credit here from the
want of hard money and the prejudice it is to our affairs—"[52] they want $20000 and are disheartened. May
8, "The Tories will not trust us a farthing . . . Our
enemies take advantage of this distress to make us look
contemptible in the eyes of Canadians who have been
provoked by the violence of our military in exacting
provisions and services from them without pay—a conduct towards a people who suffered us to enter their
country as friends that the most urgent necessity can
scarce excuse since it contributed much to the change
of their good dispositions towards us into enmity and
makes them wish our departure[53]. . . . Your Commissioners themselves are in a critical and most irksome
situation, pestered hourly with demands great and
small that they cannot answer. . . . In short if money
cannot be had to support your Army here with honour
so as to be respected instead of being hated by the
people, we report it as our firm and unanimous opinion
that it is better immediately to withdraw it . . . the
inhabitants are become enemies . . . ." Money was
needed to pay debts of £14000 and a further sum of
"hard money not less than £6000 will be necessary to
re-establish our credit in this Colony."[54]

Congress was not deaf to the call for money: May
24, 1776, Hancock writes to Schuyler that Congress was

sending him "£1662.1.3 in hard money which was all that was in the Treasury."

Schuyler had been urged by Chase and Carroll in a letter from Montreal, May 16, "For God's sake send powder and pork," and, May 17, "Press Congress to send paper money as well as specie—let the bills be small;" and, May 27, they reported to Congress that the Army was not above 4000 of whom 400 were sick—two-thirds had not had the small-pox and were liable to be stricken—"Yesterday we seized by force fifteen barrels of flour. . . . You are indebted to your troops treble $11000 and to the inhabitants above $15000."[55]

Franklin was sick in body and mind, utterly dissatisfied with the situation; and he determined to leave Montreal which he did, May 11,[56] after being in that city eleven or twelve days. The double reason given for his return was that his health was bad and he desired to make a report of the alarming situation in person. That his health was seriously affected there can be no doubt: even at Saratoga at Schuyler's he has written farewell to some of his friends: but Franklin was not the man to abandon a post for personal reasons like health if he thought he could be of service to his country by remaining—he saw the situation to be hopeless. There was great cause for alarm, news had come, May 10, of the retreat of the Colonial forces from Quebec and there was great fear of a British vessel sailing up to Montreal, the River being now open.

With Franklin went the Roman Catholic Jesuit priest, John Carroll, a relative of Charles Carroll of Carrollton, one of the Commissioners; he had been brought into Canada by and with the Commissioners pursuant to the Resolution of Congress already mentioned.

The other two Commissioners, Chase and Carroll, accompanied Franklin as far as St. Johns where they intended to stay until the military situation should clear: Franklin and the priest went on, Franklin determined to return to Philadelphia on account of his health and John Carroll considering that it was out of his power to be of any service after the Commissioners had left Montreal.

Reversing their route, they left Albany, May 22, by "Chariot which they are to take down to New York."[57] The other Commissioners were not long behind: on May 31, they left for the south and, June 11, they attended the Congress and gave an account of their proceedings and the state of the Army in Canada.[58] Thus ended in complete and decisive failure a mission from which much had been expected.

What were the reasons for this dismal failure?

Not the personnel of the Commission. Franklin was a man of mature years and intellect, without religious or other bigotry, tolerant of the views of others, an experienced and successful negotiator, accustomed to dealing with others than the English Colonist and able and willing to understand the psychology of those not his own people—his subsequent success in France proves his eminent qualifications for such a post.[58a]

Samuel Chase, of Maryland, was in the very prime of life and was one of the most conspicuous and able members of the Continental Congress: an ardent lover of liberty and justice, he was also persuasive and where possible conciliatory.[59]

Charles Carroll, of Carrollton, just under forty, had studied in France as well as London: he was well versed in the French language and understood the French people. An ardent Roman Catholic, and a landed gentleman, he was thus recommended to the Canadian noblesse and priesthood: while he could not boast of the privileges or even freedom of Roman Catholics in the Thirteen Colonies which he represented,[60] he could prove in his own person that it was possible for a Roman Catholic to attain a high and honorable position in the Congress and country. With them came John Carroll, a Roman Catholic priest, chosen by Popery-hating Congress because he was a Roman Catholic priest. He had been educated with his kinsman, Charles Carroll, at the English Jesuit College at St. Omer, France, and later studied philosophy at Liège; he entered the Society of Jesus at the age of eighteen and was ordained priest at thirty-four. On the suppression of the Society in 1773, he returned to his native Maryland where he was devoting himself to the spiritual care of his co-religionists when the summons came from his kinsman to accompany him to Canada. An amiable, cultured and polished man, sincere and devoted in his religion, he was a patriotic American; while he was under no delusion as to the difficulties of his task, he cheerfully obeyed the call of his country.[61]

Nor was the failure due to the conduct of the Commissioners.

"Received at the landing by General Arnold and a great body of officers, gentry, &c, and saluted by firing of cannon and other military honours—being conducted to the General's house . . . served with a glass of wine while people were crowding in to pay their compliments,"[62] they went to work without delay.

The priest, knowing that to win the clergy would be of most material consequence, brought with him a letter from Father Farmer, of Philadelphia, to Father Pierre Floquet, a Jesuit, and the last of the Canadian Superiors of that Mission. Floquet was a supporter of the American cause: the property of his Order had been confiscated by the British conqueror, and he naturally resented the act. There was no hope of any favorable turn in British sentiment and the only chance of relief was the success of the Americans. Carroll received permission to celebrate mass from the Vicar-General, Monsignor Mongolfier, and did so in the house of Floquet."[63]

But he failed to convince the Canadian clergy that the sentiments of the Address to the People of Great Britain were not the sentiments of the Continental Congress and of the people of the Thirteen Colonies—he could not point to any one Colony in which the Roman Catholic Church and clergy had such privileges as in Canada and he could point to only one and that not his own in which the individual Roman Catholic had the ordinary rights of a freeman.

The Commissioners themselves were equally busy. They at once went into the situation and condition of the military force as well as of Canadian sentiment; on the morning after their arrival at Montreal, they held a Council of War and decided to fortify Jacques Cartier and Deschambault and to build four row galleys or gondolas at Chambly—they even turned over some of the specie furnished for their own expenses, to pay Canadian workmen.

The army was in a very bad condition; the troops were "without bread, tents, shoes, stockings, shirts, &c"; of the 4000, some 400 were sick, some with small-pox and two-thirds had not had that fell disease and feared it. Small-pox was a very real danger: vaccination was two decades and more in the future[64]—inoculation had indeed been introduced into England by Lady Hester Stanhope some sixty years before and the practice of inoculating had spread shortly thereafter into America, but it had not proved satisfactory and had been forbidden in Massachusetts (except in Boston); and generally in the Continental Army as in the British Army it was disapproved by the authorities.[65] As regards the number of those who were sick and the lack of supplies, it was said that men who had pleaded indisposition had many of them been foremost in the flight from Quebec and had carried off on their backs "such burdens as hearty and stout men would labour under," and that they and others had left their baggage behind—but this was a little later. For much of the unfortunate condition of the troops, the Commissioners blamed General Wooster who had become Senior officer on the death of Montgomery; he, in turn, accused them of improper interference with his authority;[66] Chase and Carroll, at length, recommended his recall.[67]

Neither army nor Commissioners were responsible for the lack of supplies—John Jay recognized the justice of the common view that "the miscarriages in" Canada "are . . . attributable to the inattention of Congress." Charles Cushing who was with the Army could with knowledge and truth say: "The Army in Canada . . . have been shamefully neglected and imposed upon"[68]; and every Commander in almost every despatch complained of lack of supplies and money.

It can hardly be said with justice that Congress was oblivious of or indifferent to the situation—May 23, 1776, it was "Resolved that a Committee of five be appointed to confer with General Washington, Major General Gates and Brigadier General Mifflin upon the most speedy and effective means of supporting the American cause in Canada"—and a Committee was selected composed of John Adams, R. H. Lee, Harrison, Wilson and Rutledge. A committee had been appointed to "collect hard money for the Canadian expedition,"[69] and, May 22, 1776[70] it was "Resolved that the specie now in the Treasury and as much more as can be procured not exceeding the sum of $100,000 to be immediately remitted to the Commissioners for the payment of debts due from these Colonies in Canada and for the preservation of publick credit.

"That the Commissioners in Canada and General Schuyler be informed that we cannot give them any assurance of maintaining our army there by hard money but that this ought not to discourage our operations, Congress being determined to send from these

Colonies supplies of provisions and all other necessaries if hard money cannot be obtained and that in the meantime the best endeavours shall be used to obtain the sum of $100000 in hard money.''

The following day, May 24, 1776, Hancock was able to write the Commissioners that he was sending General Schuyler "£1662.1.3 in hard money which was all that was in the Treasury.''[71] This was, of course, too late, as the Commissioners had left Montreal by this time and had left Canada before in the ordinary course the money could reach them.[72]

If no one was to blame—certainly not the Commissioners—for the condition of affairs financially in Canada, the same cannot be said of the state of feeling of Canadians for the Americans. I do not go to any but American sources for this. Notwithstanding the protestations of Congress and of Generals, notwithstanding that the French Canadians made no resistance to the entry of the American Army into Montreal and no small or uninfluential part of the English-speaking population welcomed it, it speedily became detested.

So far as appears, no tidings had yet been brought of any misconduct on the part of Arnold's troops on the way to or at Quebec: and the Canadians in and near Montreal were to judge of Americans from personal experience.

A number of French Canadians enlisted in the American service—Moses Hazen commanded some of them.[73]

How stood the matter in a few months?

As we have seen, Congress as early as April 23, 1776, had been informed of injuries offered to Canadians by Americans and expressed their resentment and their intention to punish the offenders: and the Commissioners, May 8, 1776, reported that the Canadians had been provoked by the violence of the military in exacting provisions and services from them without pay.

Moreover acts of violence were not uncomomn against those defending their own, while property was frequently taken without payment and as frequently with payment in worthless promises.[74]

Acts of violence on the part of an English-speaking soldiery were almost unknown in Canada: a rigid discipline was exercised and swift and condign punishment inflicted for any offence of the kind by British soldiers;[75] and it was with amazement that the French-Canadians saw the violent acts of the Americans unpunished and almost unchecked.

It is also clear that notwithstanding the sincere desire of Washington and others in authority, the religion of the vast majority of Canadians and the objects of their veneration were flouted by unwise and undisciplined American soldiers. No one can possibly doubt the cordial dislike of Roman Catholicism by many and the major part of the Colonists of the Thirteen Colonies —it cannot be thought that the Address to the People of Great Britain was a piece of rhetoric and hypocrisy which did not actually express the true sentiments of the Congress and of those represented by Congress. Nor is it at all to be wondered at that this dislike on occasion manifested itself in speech and act. The priesthood were slighted and contemptuously treated— a treatment very galling to those who had been accustomed to be treated with deference amounting to reverence.

The Commissioners being guests at the Chateau de Ramezay (still in existence) had the French Printer, Mesplet, in the Chateau; his Printing Press in the Crypt printed some (only two are known) documents intended to show the good intentions toward Canadians of the Colonists to the South. Outside of the priests and the Seigneurs, there were very few except the Notaries who could read—the Seigneurs were too often treated with as little respect as the priests and the

Notaries were skilled in and devoted to the French Law so much execrated by Americans—it was not to be expected that any advantage to the cause of the Colonies would follow the use of Mesplet's Printing Press and none in fact ever did.[76]

Nor were the Commissioners much more successful with the English-speaking inhabitants of Canada. The very steps taken to ingratiate their cause with these quasi-friends proved more harmful than effective. Officers of the Canadian Militia who had been imprisoned at Chambly for refusing to resign their Commissions were set free, much to Wooster's indignation;[77] all those who had been expelled from Montreal for Loyalist sympathies were allowed to return and the exile of others ceased. All this was along the lines the recommendation of Joseph Hawley to Samuel Adams[78] to give the Canadians a full taste of liberty—but it was wholly opposed to the theory and practice of Wooster who tolerated no expression of sentiment adverse to the American cause.[79] If ever this policy of tolerance could have been successful, it was now quite too late: the English-speaking were divided into two irreconcilable and bitterly hostile parties, the Loyalists hating and despising the American faction as traitors, the latter returning the hate and contempt in full against those whom they characterized as slaves of a tyrannical government across the Sea.

Some of the officers at Montreal in presence of the Commissioners, threw their commissions on the floor and trampled them underfoot, swearing they would never again serve under men who destroyed with one stroke of the pen what they had risked their lives to obtain. One even "damn'd Mr. Chase to his face, swearing when he prayed him to accept an important command, that he would not fire another gun for the Congress till their officers and soldiers were put on an equal footing with their enemies." All in vain—"a cause that cannot support itself upon the principles of liberty is not worth pursuing. We will not do evil that good may ensue. It is a most substantial wrong to exile a man five hundred miles from his own home only because he is disaffected, &c, &c, &c.''[80] Neither persuaded the other—the Commissioners went on on their theory of liberty, the Canadian English felt betrayed and humiliated.

As early as June 11, 1776, Hancock writes to Washington: ''Mr. Chase and Mr. Carroll arrived this day: by their account there has been the most shocking mismanagement in that quarter,'' i.e., Canada:[81] July 1, John Adams laments to Samuel Chase, ''Alas Canada! We have found misfortune and disgrace in that quarter . . . evacuated at last,''[82] while, June 17, Josiah Bartlett states to John Langdon,[83] ''Dr. Franklin, Mr. Chase and Mr. Carroll are returned from Canada. Their account of the behaviour of our New England officers and soldiers touches me to the quick—by their account never men behaved so badly.''

Congress could not pass the matter over: a Committee was appointed to examine into the causes of the failure of the attempt to bring Canada in line with the Thirteen Colonies: July 30, 1776, the Committee reported the reasons as 1—Short enlistment of Continental Troops: 2—Want of hard money and 3—A still greater and more fatal source of misfortunes the prevalence of small-pox.[84]

All these had their influence; but the Committee failed to mention a more important cause for which Congress was itself responsible, namely the bitter attack upon the Roman Catholic religion in the Address to the People of Great Britain. No Address to Canadians, no special pleading of Commissioners, no assurance of Commanders, could persuade the clerical leaders in Canada that Congress did not mean what it said in that Address.

Accordingly, the Clergy headed by the energetic and very able Bishop Briand of Quebec, remained firm in their allegiance to the British Crown. Nothing but very strong reasons could induce the Laity to decline to follow their Clergy: and no such reasons ever appeared but rather the reverse. Their goods taken and service compelled by force; even where payment was in form made, it was so made in worthless paper—there was nothing to induce them to take to their arms the hereditary foe. Under the Quebec Act they had the government and the laws to which they were accustomed and with which they were content, and no prospect was held out for anything more agreeable to their wishes.

As we have seen, the Commissioners were not more successful with the English-speaking part of the community, small as it was.

Under the circumstances, the task was beyond human powers, and no discredit can attach to the failure of Franklin and his colleagues.

WILLIAM RENWICK RIDDELL.

Osgoode Hall, Toronto,
    October 2, 1923.

REFERENCES.

[1] These Articles will be found in Shortt and Doughty's *Documents relating to the Constitutional History of Canada, 1759–1791*, Ottawa, 1918, 2d Ed. (hereinafter cited "S. & D."), pp. 7, 25—a most valuable collection.

[2] S. & D., pp. 99, 100, 115. Of the inhabitants before the Conquest, a very small proportion were Protestant: the Archivist of Quebec, M. Pierre George Roy, a competent authority, says: "Sous l'ancien régime très peu de protestants eurent la chance de s'établir au Canada." See his *Le Vieux Quebec*, Quebec, 1923, at p. 151; of the Protestant French not more than two became prominent, Francis Mounet, who was made a Legislative Councillor, and Pierre Du Calvet, who became a traitor but escaped more than suspicion. He was imprisoned by Haldimand and was afterwards lost at sea.

Benjamin Franklin's Mission to Canada.

[3] See Report of the Lords of Trade, November 5, 1761, upon the proposal to transport a number of Germans to the American Colonies after the peace: the Southern Colonies were less populated, S. & D., p. 162, n. 2.

[4] S. & D., pp. 163, sqq.

[5] Report, Lords of Trade, June 8, 1763, S. & D., pp. 132, sqq., esp. pp. 138, 139, 140, 141 and 142.

[6] S. & D., pp. 173, sqq.

[7] S. & D., pp. 181, sqq.

[8] See also Letter, Earl of Egremont, Secretary of State, to Murray, Aug. 13, 1763, S. & D., pp. 168-9: Canadian Archives, Q. 1, p. 117.

[9] That would probably have taken place had it not been for the "Canada Pamphlet," 1760-1761, of Franklin, then representing the Province of Pennsylvania at London. See my article, "The Status of Canada," Am. Bar Assn. Journal, June, 1921; also my Address "Franklin and Canada," Empire Club, Toronto, November 15, 1923.

[10] I am speaking generally: a few French Canadians seem to have wished for an Assembly—a few English and Americans were content with the existing form of Government.

[11] Letter, Murray to Lords of Trade, Quebec, Oct. 29, 1764: S. & D., p. 231, Can. Arch., Q. 2, p. 233.

[12] Letter, Murray to Earl of Shelburne (afterwards first Marquis of Lansdowne), Quebec, Aug. 30, 1766. Can. Arch., Shelburne Correspondence, vol. 64, p. 101.

[13] With the possible exception of a few of the noblesse, the French Canadians were satisfied with the English Criminal Law—barbarous as it was, it was less so than their own—and the French Criminal Law was never reintroduced.

[14] The Act is (1774) 14 George 3, c. 83 (Imp); S. & D., pp. 570-576.

[15] This is usually printed as Sec. 2 of the Quebec Act.

[16] Section 7 relieves Roman Catholics from the oath required by (1558) 1 Eliz. c. 1, s. 19: and substitutes one less but at the same time sufficiently drastic.

[17] Section 12 of the Act.

[18] Section 8: "Laws of Canada" means "Laws of Canada before the Conquest."

[19] Apparently January 13, 1774.

[20] Peter Force's ponderous volumes of "American Archives" (hereinafter cited "Am. Arch."), Ser. IV, Vol. 1, p. 627. Perhaps another letter may be of interest. An "American" writes Lord North, London, February 5, 1774: "As an American, give me leave to assure your Lordship that I think the dismissal of Dr. Franklin from the P.M. General in N. A. at this particular crisis one of the most fortunate events that could have happened for that Country . . . the people there never liked the institution and only acquiesced in it out of their unbounded affection for the person that held the office . . . thus will happily end your boasted Post Office so often given as a precedent for taxing the Americans." do. do. p. 501. As is well-known,

Benjamin Franklin's Mission to Canada.

Benjamin Franklin was the Deputy Postmaster General for America—the first to be appointed—and dismissed for his activities.

[21] Journals of the Continental Congress, Vol. 1, pp. 34–35: Am. Arch., Ser. IV, Vol. 1, p. 905. It is to be remembered that this Resolution was passed when "the Colonies hold in abhorrence the idea of being considered independent communities on the British Government." The indignation against the "establishment" of the Roman Catholic Church did not proceed from abhorrence of the principle of establishment itself but from hatred of Roman Catholicism—for many years after the Revolution a citizen of Connecticut had to pay to support the Congregational minister unless he could "sign off" by stating that he belonged to another church. See my Article, "Common Law and Common Sense," 27 Yale Law Journal (June, 1918), p. 798, n. 12. The example is given of such a certificate: "I, J. S., hereby certify that I have ceased to be a Christian and have joined the Episcopal Church."

The Suffolk meeting was a meeting of the Delegates of every Town and District of the County of Suffolk held on Tuesday, September 6, 1774, at the hour of Mr. Richard Woodward, of Dedham, and by adjournment at the house of Mr. Voge, of Milton, on Friday, September 9, 1774—Joseph Palmer, Esq., being chosen President and William Thompson, Esq., Clerk. Am. Arch., Series IV, Vol. 1, p. 776.

[22] Am. Arch., Ser. IV, Vol. 1, p. 910. "All which Statutes are impolitick, unjust and cruel as well as unconstitutional and most dangerous and destructive of American rights." The Convention of Pennsylvania, July 15, 1774, had resolved that "unconditional independence on the parent state is abhorrent to our principles"—and freely acknowledged allegiance to Great Britain, do. do., p. 555. September 28, 1774, Mr. Galloway's motion was carried: "that the Colonies hold in abhorrence the idea of being considered independent communities on the British Government." do. do., p. 905.

[23] Am. Arch., Ser. IV, Vol. 1, p. 914.

[24] I have not met the phrase "dominion of Canada" in any earlier document—of course the present "Dominion of Canada" has no reference to this Address. The Address will be found in Am. Arch., Ser. IV, Vol. 1, p. 920—in an earlier part of the same Address the Congress had said: "We think the Legislature is not authorized by constitution to establish a religion fraught with sanguinary and impious tenets or to erect an arbitary form of government in any quarter of the globe."

[25] For John Dickinson, see The Life and Times of John Dickinson prepared at the request of the Historical Society of Pennsylvania by Charles Stille—Printed for the Society, Philadelphia, 1891-5: he was aptly termed "The Pen of the Revolution" and was the first to advocate opposition to the ministerial plan of taxation on constitutional grounds. John Adams seems to have thought him, "a peddling genius." See Letter, John Adams to James Warren, Philadelphia, July 24, 1775, Can. Arch., B 27, p. 349.

[26] Am. Arch., Ser. IV, Vol. I, pp. 930, 934. Kingsford's History of Canada, Vol. V, pp. 262-7.

Benjamin Franklin's Mission to Canada.

[27] Do. do. do., p. 934.

[28] See the Letter from a gentleman of Montreal, January 18, 1775, Am. Arch., Ser. IV, Vol. I, p. 1164—the writer says "the French Bourgeois . . . have been so little accustomed to speak or think on subjects of that kind and are so much afraid of giving the smallest offence to Government that they will avoid taking any part in the matter. The noblesse enter very sanguinely into the scheme of raising troops, but the priests we are well assured will disapprove of it."

[29] Can. Arch., Q 11, p. 129. Carleton left Quebec about October 1, 1775, for Montreal after he had made every effort to induce the Canadians to join him. Fortifications were put in an immediate state of repair, and there was great consternation—See Letter to a Gentleman of London from Quebec, October 1, 1775. Am. Arch., Series IV, Vol. 3, p. 925—Washington in a letter to Schuyler, October 4, 1775, says that Captain Gamble writing to General Gage and Major Sheriff says "that if Quebec should be attacked before Carleton can throw himself into it, there will be a surrender without firing a shot," do. do. do., p. 945.

[30] In Carleton's letter to Dartmouth, Quebec, May 15, 1755. Can. Arch., Q 11, p. 164.

[31] In same letter: "Brown" was John Brown as to whom see Prof. Justin H. Smith's *Our Struggle for the Fourteenth Colony*, Putnams, New York and London, 1907, Vol. 1,—90, sqq.

[32] The common name for the New Englanders and those from the Thirteen Colonies generally among the French Canadians was "Bostonais." It may be of interest to quote French-Canadian Dictionaries on the word. *Le Parler Populaire des Canadiens Français* by Dr. N. E. Dionne, Quebec, 1909, says *sub. voc.* "Bastonais:" "Bostonais, citoyen de la ville de Boston. Sous le régime français, les *Bastonais*, c'est-à-dire les Anglais de la Nouvelle-Angleterre, étaient fort redoutés de nos Canadiens." The author might have added that by reason of repeated raids on each other's territory, "nos Canadiens" and "les Bastonais" hated each other a little more than they hated the devil. Indeed the New England divine to impress his flock with the terrors of hell compared the devil and his angels to the French Canadian invaders.

Dictionaire Canadien-Français by Sylva Clapin, Montreal and Boston, n.d., is a little more full. "Bastonais . . . pour Bostonais ou Bostonien, habitant de Boston. Au temps des anciennes luttes, armeés dirigées en Amérique par l'élément anglais contre les Franco-Canadiens, plus tard, lors des démêlés avec les Etats-Unis, les plans d'attaque se préparaient dans la Nouvelle-Angleterre et plus particulièrement dans son centre le plus important, c.-à-d, Boston.

De là, le nom de *Bostonais* et, par corruption, de Bastonais, donné a tous ceux, que dans le temps s'avançaient du sud, en ennemis, vers les frontières canadiennes. Dans la suite, et la légende brodant sur le tout, *Bastonais* devint synonyme de quelque chose de particulièrement terrible et violent, et plus d'une mère canadienne put apaiser de longues années durant, la turbulence de son enfant, en agitant devant ses yeux ce farouche spectre, en guise de Croquemitaine."

Benjamin Franklin's Mission to Canada.

The former passage translated reads: "Bostonais, citizen of the City of Boston. In the French regime, the *Bastonais*, *i.e.*, the English of New England, were much dreaded by our Canadians"—
The latter: "Bastonais for Bostonais or Bostonian an inhabitant of Boston. During the time of the old armed struggles in America by the English element and the French Canadians and later on during the conflicts with the United States, the plans of attack were prepared in New England and more particularly in Boston, its most important centre. For that reason the name 'Bostonais', by corruption 'Bastonais', was given to all who at those times advanced from the South as enemies towards the Canadian frontiers. Later on, the story being embellished, *Bastonais* became a synonym for anything particularly terrible and violent, and more than one Canadian mother for many years was able to quiet the turbulence of her child by brandishing that wild spectre as a bugbear before its eyes."

[33] Can. Arch., Q 11, p. 196, in Carleton's letter to Dartmouth from Montreal, June 7, 1775: Can. Arch., Q 11, p. 184. The same letter reports that Benedict Arnold, a native of Connecticut and a horse jockey, had surprised St. John's—that the rebels under Arnold (500 men, 1500 volunteers on the way) had surprised Ticonderoga and Crown Point—a party under Ethan Allen, an outlaw from New York, remained at St. John's.

[34] These despatches are copied with very great care—the copyist makes the word read "Prinkins"—possibly "Redskins".

[35] Shelburne Papers (Can. Arch.), Vol. 66, p. 53. Francis Maseres was appointed Attorney General of the Province of Quebec in March, 1766, but returned to England in 1769: he afterwards became Cursitor Baron of the Exchequer. His works on mathematics, especially on the Minus sign, are still worth reading.

[36] The same kind of reasoning was at the bottom of the strenuous objection to the use of Coloured Troops during the Revolutionary and Civil Wars.

[37] Shelburne Papers (Can. Arch.), Vol. 66, p. 53.

[38] E. g., Guilday: *"The Life and Times of John Carroll,"* N. Y., 1922: Tetu: *"Notices Biographivues des Evêques de Quebec,"* Quebec, 1889. Gosselin: *"L'Eglise du Canada après la Conquête."*

[39] Am. Arch., Ser. IV, Vol. 2, pp. 1038, 1833 and 1836. Dickinson and Mifflin were appointed a Committee to get this Address translated into French and have 1000 copies sent to Canada for distribution. do. do. do., p. 1039.
A Canadian is reminded of the vain-glorious Proclamation of General Hull, July 12, 1812, when he invaded Upper Canada. If the Canadians are good, "You will be emancipated from tyranny and oppression, and restored to the dignified station of freemen." This Proclamation is generally attributed to Lewis Cass.

[40] Congress had determined, June 1, 1775, that "No expedition or incursion ought to be undertaken or made by any Colony or body of Colonies against or into Canada:" and, June 27, 1775, it was resolved

that Major General Schuyler should obtain the best intelligence he could
of the disposition of the Canadians and Indians of Canada, and "that
if General Schuyler finds it practicable and that it will not be dis-
agreeable to the Canadians he do immediately take possession of St.
Johns, Montreal and any other parts of the country." do. do. do., pp.
1845, 1855. The Canadians were not consulted as to Arnold's expedition
to Quebec.

[41] Am. Arch., Ser. IV, Vol. 3, pp. 763, 4, 5.

[42] I venture to think that sufficient attention has not been given by
historians to this extraordinary Anabasis and Catabasis by Arnold—
if it had a Xenophon, the story would rival in interest that of the Ten
Thousand. The story of the escape of Carleton from Montreal to Quebec
is also a thrilling one—"a favourable wind the night before (*i.e.*, November 11, 1775) enabled Mr. Carleton to get away with his little garrison
on board ten or eleven little vessels reserved for that purpose, and to
carry away the powder and other important stores." Montgomery to
Schuyler, Montreal, November 13, 1775. Am. Arch., Ser. IV, Vol. 3,
p. 1602. Schuyler in his despatch to the President of the Congress
from Ticonderoga, November 27, 1775, says:—"I am informed that all
the vessels in which Mr. Carleton had embarked himself, his Troops,
and stores have surrendered by capitulation—that Carleton got on
shore and was gone toward Quebeck," Am. Arch., Ser. IV, Vol. 3, p.
1682. The next day he adds: "General Carleton stole from aboard the
vessels with six Canadians and dressed like one of them: in this disguise he hopes to get into Quebeck; but if he does, the weather has
been so severe that I trust he will not be able to leave it, and then
he must fall into our hands in the course of the winter if not immediately," do. do. do., p. 1682. This hope proved vain and with tremendous
results. See an account of this thrilling adventure in Kingsford's
History of Canada, Vol. V, pp. 462, 3. In his letter to the citizens
of Montreal on his taking possession of the city, November 12, 1775,
Montgomery says that it was "falsely and scandalously reported that
our intentions are to plunder the inhabitants," do. do., p. 1596.

[43] Am. Arch., Ser. IV, Vol. 4, p. 1653.

[44] Am. Arch., Ser. IV, Vol. 5, p. 1692: do. do. do., p. 1689.

[45] Dr. John Fothergill, a physician and scientist of note, wrote in
1765, a pamphlet now quite rare, "Considerations relative to the North
American Colonies," in which he advocated the repeal of the Stamp Act.
In 1774, he collaborated with Franklin in drawing up a scheme of
reconciliation: this unfortunately was never taken seriously by the
Government. Fothergill is still remembered in medical circles as the
first to recognize the specific character of diphtheria: he was a Quaker
and very charitable—he gave away about £200,000. D.N.B., Vol. XX,
p. 66, Bass, Hist. Med., pp. 651, 657, 719, 739.

[46] Am. Arch., Ser. IV, Vol. 2, pp. 178–1820.

[47] Do. do. do., p. 455.

[48] Do. do. do., p. 1771.

[49] (Sir) Guy Carleton (afterwards Lord Dorchester) Governor of

Benjamin Franklin's Mission to Canada.

Quebec, *i.e.*, Canada, 1768-1778, a man of great energy and ability: had such as he been Governors of the Thirteen Colonies, there might have been no Revolution; none would have been needed, the wishes of the Colonists would have been listened to sympathetically: he was the real author of the Quebec Act.

[50] Am. Arch., Ser. IV, p. 411.

[51] Do. do., p. 1650—they were to render an account.

[52] Am. Arch., Ser. IV, Vol. 5, p. 1166; Can. Arch., B 27, p. 389: Smith, *op. cit.*, p. 341, gives a *facsimile* of part of this Despatch. Immediately after the words quoted, we find "Not the most trifling service can be procured without an assurance of instant pay in silver or gold. The express we sent from St. Johns to inform the General of our arrival there and to request carriages for La Prairie was not at the ferry till a friend, passing, changed a dollar for us into silver and we are obliged to that friend, Mr. McCartney, for his engagement to pay the calashes or they would not have been furnished." The Commissioners after staying a stort time with Schuyler at Saratoga had proceeded to Ticonderoga, which they reached in ten days: thence on water three days—landing at night to sleep—to St. Johns: thence by caleche to La Prairie and down the River to Montreal, which they reached in twenty-seven days from New York.

[53] Tuesday, April 23, 1776, on the Report of a Committee, Congress "Resolved that the Commission from Congress to Canada be desired to publish an Address to the People of Canada signifying that Congress has been informed of injuries offered by our people to some of them expressing their resentment at their conduct: assuring them of our attachment to their security, inviting them to state their grievances to our Commissioners and promising ample redress to them and punishment to the offenders.

" Resolved that Instructions be sent to the Commissioners to cause justice to be done to the Canadians agreeable to the above resolve." do. do., 1686. No justice was done to Canadians or punishment to the offenders. I cannot find that any such Address was published; if so, it was a dead letter.

[54] Do. do., pp. 1166, 1237: Can. Arch., B 27, p. 389. The Commissioners had been expected to bring "hard money" with them, but they had not done so—apparently not even a dollar. See note 52 supra.

Franklin himself says in his "Sketch of the Services of B. Franklin to the United States of America" that "in Canada . . . he . . . advanced to General Arnold and other servants of Congress, then in extreme distress, £353 in gold, out of his own pocket, on the credit of Congress, which was of great service at that juncture, in procuring provisions for our army." John Bigelow; *The Life of Benjamin Franklin*, London, 1879, Vol. 3, pp. 424, 425.

[55] Am. Arch., Ser. IV, Vol. 6, pp. 558, 578, 586, 590.

[56] Do. do., p. 587, Chase and Carroll's despatch to Hancock from Montreal, May 17, 1776. Carleton in his Despatch to Germain, Quebec, May 14, 1776, says that intelligence received at Quebec that day from

Benjamin Franklin's Mission to Canada.

Montreal from a person who had never deceived, was that Franklin had gone off with Mrs. Walker and Mrs. Price. Can. Arch., Q 12, p. 22.

[57] Letter John Carroll to Charles Carroll, Sr., Philadelphia, June 2, 1776. Rowland *Life and Correspondence of Charles Carroll of Carrollton*, Vol. 1, pp. 170, 171: Guilday's *Life and Times of John Carroll*, New York, 1922, pp. 103, 104.

Despatch from Fort George, May 28, 1776. Am. Arch., Ser. IV, Vol. 6, p. 610.

[58] Am. Arch., Ser. IV, Vol. 6, p. 1702—see also do. do. do., pp. 493, 587, 589.

[58a] Since this paper was written I have seen the characterization of Benjamin Franklin by Dr. Nicholas Murray Butler in his very able and illuminating work, *Building the American Nation*, N. Y., Charles Scribner's Sons, 1923. This is a collection of the Lectures on the Sir George Watson Foundation for American History, Literature and Institution delivered by the President of Columbia University in the summer of 1923 in England, Scotland and Wales; and is "an impressive interpretation of the origin of the American nation largely in terms of the individuals who formed it."

Full justice is done to Franklin's gentleness, persuasiveness, large human sympathy, his restless intellectual activity, his imagination and his wide range of thought. Condorcet's picture of him is quoted with deserved approval:

> "L'humanité et la franchise étaient la base de sa morale; une gaieté habituelle, une douce facilité dans la vie commune, une inflexibilité tranquille dans les affaires importantes formaient son caractère.
>
> *Œuvres de Condorcet*, (Paris, 1847), III, 415–416."

The first chapter of Dr. Butler's interesting and valuable book contains an admirable account of Benjamin Franklin and Samuel Adams, which invites and will bear reading again and again.

[59] His conduct as Chief Justice of Maryland was without reproach: and his Impeachment as Justice of the Supreme Court of the United States did little credit to the Party responsible for it. His acquittal is one pregnant example of the sense of justice of a free people.

[60] "Everywhere, except in Pennsylvania to be a Catholic, was to cease to possess full civil rights and privileges." Guilday, *op. cit.*, pp. 70, 71.

In many parts of the Thirteen Colonies "a Protestant family ran a fearful risk in harboring a Romanist." Shea's *History of the Catholic Church in the United States*, N. Y. 1890, p. 498. Even after the Declaration of Independence, which is very generally supposed to have put an end to this religious intolerance, the *New England Primer* which was put in the hands of very many children had cuts of the "Man of Sin." The edition of 1779 contains a picture of the martyrdom by burning of John Rogers in 1554 and the statement: "A few days before his death he wrote the following advice to his children 'Abhor the arrant whore of Rome and all her blasphemies, and drink not of her

Benjamin Franklin's Mission to Canada.

cup; obey not her decrees.'" See Paul Leicester Ford's *The New England Primer:* Riley's *The Founder of Mormonism*, London, 1903.

The mutual tolerance in old Quebec of Protestant and Catholic has been underrated: While there was almost from the beginning, certainly from 1763, a strong anti-English and anti-French feeling there never was any anti-Protestant and anti-Catholic feeling. As is well known, Lord Durham in his celebrated Report, 1838—which showed the state of society in Lower Canada after decades of dispute and recrimination between French and English—was (somewhat to his own astonishment) able to say: "It is indeed an admirable feature of Canadian society that it is entirely devoid of any religious dissensions. Sectarian intolerance is not merely not avowed, but it hardly seems to influence men's feelings." Lucas' *Lord Durham's Report*, Oxford, 1912, vol. i, pp. 239, 240, vol. ii, p. 39. And this when Harriet Martineau in her *Society in America* 4th Edit., 1837, vol. ii, p. 322, could say: "Parents put into their children's hands as religious books, foul libels against the Catholics which are circulated throughout the country. In the west I happened to find a book of this kind which no epithet but 'filthy' will describe." Qu.? *Maria Monk's Awful Disclosures*, 1836.

There are so many who, as Morley says of Froude,—*Recollections by John Viscount Morley*, Toronto, 1917, Vol. 1, p. 280—"think the quarrel between Protestant and Catholic the only thing in the universe that matters," and they think anyone contemptible who with Daniel O'Connell can say: "Every religion is good, every religion is true—to him who in his due caution and conscience believes it. There is but one bad religion, that of a man who professes a faith which he does not believe; but the good religion may be, and often is, corrupted by the wretched and wicked prejudices which admit a difference of opinion as a cause of hatred."

[61] The life and labours of John Carroll, Archbishop of Baltimore, have been commemorated in many works, *e.g.* Brent, *Biographical Sketch* . . . , Baltimore, 1843: Shea's *History of the Roman Catholic Church in the U. S.* A worthy memorial is at last presented by Guilday's *Life and Times of John Carroll* . . . N. Y., 1922, an accurate and well-written book, of which I have made full use.

[62] Letter from John Carroll to his mother, Montreal, May 1, 1776, Brent, *op. cit.*, pp. 40–43: Guilday, *op. cit.*, pp. 101, 102: Am. Arch., Ser. V, Vol. 5, p. 1167: Kingsford's *History of Canada*, Vol. VI, p. 65.

[63] For this, Floquet was suspended in June, 1776, *a divinis* by Bishop Briand who charged him with seeming justice with having a *Bastonnais* heart. Floquet submitted and was reinstated, but died next year, the last of the Canadian Jesuit Superiors. Guilday, *op. cit.*, pp. 102, 103.

[64] Jenner did not begin his experiments on cow-pox until 1769: and he published his first work on vaccination in 1798. It was not until September 2, 1776, that General Gates was able to write the President of the Congress from Ticonderoga: "Thank Heavens, the small pox is totally eradicated from amongst us, not I can assure you without much vigilance and authority being previously exercised. Am. Arch., Ser. VI, Vol. 3, p. 1267.

Benjamin Franklin's Mission to Canada.

[65] John Adams, writing from Philadelphia, July 7, 1776, says: "I hope that measures will be taken to cleanse the army at Crown Point from the smallpox, and that other measures may be taken in New England by tolerating and encouraging inoculation to render that distemper less troublesome." Am. Arch., Ser. V, Vol. 3, p. 1035. The Council of Massachusetts, writing to General Artemas Ward, Watertown, July 9, 1776, says: "The Board was this day informed that you had given liberty to a number of Continental troops now stationed at Winter Hill to receive the small-pox by inoculation. The Board are unwilling to credit such a report as there is an Act of the Colony prohibiting inoculation except in the town of Boston . . . (we) desire your Honour would not permit any of the troops . . . to receive the small-pox by inoculation in any other town except the town of Boston," do. do. do., p. 146.

See also Letter, General Artemas Ward to His Excellency, Boston, July 15, 1766: do. do. do., p. 48.

Governor Trumbull, writing to the Massachusetts Council from Lebanon, August 21, 1776, says: "inoculating for small-pox which has been fallen into by the troops from your State . . . everyway hurts the public service and exposes the troops to that infection. . . ." Am. Arch., Ser. V, Vol. 1, p. 1100. Charles Cushing, writing to his brother from Crown Point, July 8, 1776, says: "The New England forces (got to Sorel) began to be very uneasy about the small-pox spreading among them as but a few of them had it. It was death for any doctor who attempted inoculation. However it was practised secretly as they were willing to run any hazard rather than take it in the natural way. Some inoculated themselves and several officers and myself began it in our own Regiment of Sorel . . . ;" (at Montreal) "the Regiment in general were inoculated for the small-pox." Am. Arch., Ser. V, Vol. 3, p. 129. Others were equally disobedient. General Schuyler, writing to the Congress from Albany, August 26, 1776, says: "Some of the militia from the eastward have inoculated themselves on the march to Skenesborough: that a number of carpenters from Rhode Island have done the same at Skenesborough. I shall instantly write to General Gates on the subject and direct that none of them be suffered to join the army to prevent this terrible disease from again destroying us." do. do. do., p. 984. Major Hawley reports to the Massachusetts Council, July 13, 1776, the men from Northampton, Massachusetts, had "a vehement desire to take small-pox by inoculation before they march." do. do. do., p. 263: August 5, 1776, he reports: "The Granville men and Branford men who have enlisted are without any orders gone into inoculation." do. do. do., p. 779. September 28, 1775, the Committee of Safety of New York would not allow William Powell to have his wife inoculated for the small-pox, as the Congress of the Province had passed a Resolution against it. do. do. do., p. 916.

[66] Wooster, in his communication to the Committee of Congress, Philadelphia, July 5, 1776, says: "The honourable Commissioners from

Benjamin Franklin's Mission to Canada.

Congress on their arrival in Canada did *ex officio* supersede my orders and released the above mentioned persons (Col. Dupee, Major Gray, and St. George Dupree) to go to Montreal where Major Gray put on his sword and cockade and strutted around like a victorious conqueror." Am. Arch., Ser. V, Vol. 1, p. 12.

[67] "General Wooster is in our opinion unfit, totally unfit, to command your Army and conduct the war . . . His stay in this Colony is unnecessary and ever prejudicial to our affairs." Despatch to Congress, May 17, 1776, Am. Arch., Ser. IV, Vol. 6., p. 589. Wooster, who had taken second place to General John Thomas, became leader again when Thomas was stricken with small-pox. do. do. do., pp. 587, 593.

[68] Letter, John Jay to Edward Rutledge, New York, July 6, 1776. Am. Arch., Ser. V, Vol. 1, p. 40.

Letter from Charles Cushing to his brother from Camp at Crown Point, July 8, 1776, do. do. do., p. 131; as to the shocking condition of the American troops at Quebec, see a Report, "Headquarters at Quebec," March 28, 1776, Can. Arch., B. 27, p. 380—this also deals with small-pox at Quebec.

Am. Arch., Ser. IV, Vol. 6, p. 1681.

[69] See Letter of Daniel Hopkins to James Warren, November ?, 1775, do. Ser. V, Vol. 3, p. 508.

[70] Do., Ser. IV, Vol. 6, p. 1679.

[71] Am. Arch., Ser. IV, Vol. 6, p. 558—the letter was written from Philadelphia, May 24, 1776.

[72] It cannot be said that finance was the strong side of Congress or that the people generally gave any creditable financial backing to the schemes of Congress. One Philadelphia banker now almost unknown to fame did as much for the finances of the nascent nation as nearly all others put together—without adequate reward, be it said.

[73] Moses Hazen writes to Antill from Montreal, March 10, 1775, that recruiting is going on slowly and that he hopes Antill has been more successful at Quebec—he suggests that the men brought by Duggan from below Quebec be re-enlisted and formed into separate companies, etc., etc. Can. Arch., B 27, p. 387. A Commission as Captain of a Company of Acadians and French Canadians was ordered to be given to Prudhome la Jeunesse, of Montreal, by the Board of War, August 21, 1776. Am. Arch., Ser. V, Vol. 1, p. 1094. See Hazen's Proclamation in French, Montreal, February 10, 1776. Can. Arch., B 27, p. 385, the engagement of his volunteers, do. do. do., p. 397.

[74] Charles Cushing in the Letter already cited, writing from the Camp at Crown Point, July 8, 1776. Am. Arch., Ser. V, Vol. 1, p. 132, says: "Our Army have very much imposed upon the inhabitants: and promised them what they could never perform, which will set them against us"—he was right.

Some evidence of illusage of the habitants and priests may be given from American Sources.

Col. Moses Hazen, writing to General Schuyler, April 1, 1776, Am. Arch., Ser. IV, 5, 869, after stating the changed feeling of Canadians towards the Americans, says:

Benjamin Franklin's Mission to Canada.

"Their clergy have been neglected and sometimes ill-used: . . . the peasantry in general have been ill-used; they have in some instances been dragooned, with the point of the bayonet, to furnish wood for the garrison at a lower rate than the current price;" half of the imperfect certificates given in payment being moreover later dishonored by the Quarter-Master General. Hazen encloses as evidence of his representations a letter from one Captain Goforth of the Continental force, commanding at Three Rivers, detailing outrages committed by the troops on their march to Quebec. "A priest's house (Goforth writes) has been entered with great violence, and his watch plundered from him. At another house they ran in debt about 20sh. and because the man wanted to be paid, run him through the neck with a bayonet. Women and children have been terrified, and forced, with the point of the bayonet, to furnish horses for private soldiers without any prospect of pay."

General Schuyler himself says to Washington in his letter from Fort George, April 27, 1776; Am. Arch., Ser. IV, 5, 1098:

"The licentiousness of our troops, both in Canada and in this quarter, is not easily described; nor have all my efforts been able to put a stop to those scandalous excesses."

May 10, 1776, Sullivan writes to Washington, Am. Arch., Ser. IV, 6, 413:

"The licentiousness of some of the troops that are gone on has been such that few of the inhabitants have escaped abuse either in their persons or property . . . Courtmartials are vain where officers connive at the depredations of the men."

In Henry's *Account of the Campaign against Quebec*, Albany, 1877, p. 98, we find an account of the sacking by the troops of the house of a prominent Canadian near Quebec: the author proceeds:

"Though our Company was composed of freeholders, or the sons of such, bred at home under the strictures of religion and morality, yet when the reins of decorum were loosed, and the honourable feeling awakened, it became impossible to administer restraint. The person of a tory, or his property, became fair game, and this at the denunciation of abase domestic villain."

Bancroft, Vol. 4, p. 376, says:

"The Canadian peasantry had been forced to furnish wood and other articles at less than the market price, or for certificates, and felt themselves outraged by the arbitrariness of the military occupation."

[75] For example, General Murray on the capitulation of Quebec at once divided the City into Quarters, where he stationed officers to whom the inhabitants might complain: every complaint was followed by immediate Court Martial, and Court Martial by immediate punishment. He notes in his Official Diary under date, November 16, 1759, "A soldier of the 48th having been tried and convicted to-day of Robbing a French Inhabitant, the Instant it was Reported the sentence was put in Execution (by hanging), in order if possible to put a stop to the Scene of Villainies which had been carried on." Can. Arch., M. 221, p. 38.

Benjamin Franklin's Mission to Canada.

In the same Diary, November 14, 1759: "As drunkeness and theft continued to reign prominent vices in the garrison highly prejudicial to the service, I recalled all licenses and ordered for the future every man found drunk to receive twenty Lashes every morning till he acknowledged where he got it and forfeit his allowance of Rum for six weeks." do. do. do., p. 38.

[76] Fleury Mesplet remained behind when the American Troops left Canada: he in 1778 applied for leave to publish a weekly paper— Can. Arch., B. 185, 1, p. 73—and started the *Montreal Gazette* (still in existence), June 3 of that year: he opposed the Government as much as he dared: in his paper he published an attack on the Judiciary as acting unjustly and in disregard of law and right; and he was in 1779 imprisoned with Jotard, his principal writer, and Du Calvet, said to have been unjustly dealt with. Can. Arch., B. 205, p. 45: do. do., B. 185, 1, p. 90. The paper was printed on the press brought from Philadelphia in the old Chateau on Notre Dame Street near Jacques Cartier Square, where it is still shown to visitors.

John Bigelow in his *Life of Benjamin Franklin*, London, 1879, Vol. 2, p. 359 (n) says:

"A printing press and printing apparatus, with hands competent to print in French and English, accompanied this mission. Two papers were issued, when it was ascertained that only one Canadian in five hundred could read. The Doctor very wisely suggested, when he returned, that if another mission was to be sent to Canada, it should consist of schoolmasters."

[77] See note 66 *ante*.

[78] Letter, Hawley to Adams, November 12, 1775, S. Adams Papers: see Smith, *op. cit.*, Vol. 2, pp. 340 sqq.

[79] How far unpopular opinion and action were tolerated in the Colonies may be illustrated by one example gloatingly retailed by Patriots of the time and given in Am. Arch., Ser. IV, Vol. 3, p. 825, under date September, 1775. James Smith, a Judge of the Court of Common Pleas for Dutchess County, New York, was Saturday, September 16 "very handsomely tarred and feathered for acting in open Contempt of the Resolves of the County Committee as was John Smith, of the same place, for like behaviour: they were carted five or six miles into the country. The Judge undertook to sue for and recover the arms taken from the Tories by order of said Committee, who assisted in disarming the Tories, which enraged the people so much that they rose and rescued the prisoners and poured out their resentment on this villainous retailer of the law." This needs no comment.

[80] See the whole story entertainingly told in Smith, *op. cit.*, pp. 340 sqq. This is a valuable and interesting work, somewhat marred by its pseudo-Carlylean style, which constantly distracts the attention from the matter to the manner. The book deserves to be better known.

[81] Letter from John Hancock to Washington, Philadelphia, June 11, 1776. Am. Arch., Ser. IV, Vol. 6, p. 812.

[82] Letter John Adams to Samuel Chase, Philadelphia, July 1, 1776, do. do. do., p. 1194.

Benjamin Franklin's Mission to Canada.

[83] Letter, Josiah Bartlett to John Langdon, Philadelphia, June 17. do. do. do., p. 1028.

[84] Am. Arch., Ser. V, Vol. 1, p. 1594: cf. pp. 1596, 1598.

NOTE.

It may be of interest to add here what has been said of Franklin's mission by some Canadian writers.

François-Xavier Garneau: *Histoire du Canada*, 5th revised ed., Paris, 1920, Vol 2, p. 343.

"Le Congrès . . . adopta diverses résolutions, dans lesquelles étaient exposés les griefs des colonies. Parmi ces griefs il plaça l'Acte de Québec. . . . 'Nous sommes étonnés . . . qu'un Parlement britannique ait consenti à donner une existence légale à une religion qui a inondé l'Angleterre de sang, et répandu l'hypocrisie, la persécution, le meurtre et la révolte dans toutes les parties du monde.' Ce langage n'aurait été que fanatique, si ceux qui le tenaient eussent été sérieux: il était insensé et puéril dans la bouche d'hommes qui songeaient alors à inviter les Canadiens à embrasser leur cause et à conquérir avec eux l'independance de l'Amérique. Cette partie de la déclaration ne produisit aucun bien en Angleterre et fit peut-être perdre le Canada à la cause de la confédération. En se déclarant contre les lois françaises et contre la religion catholique, le Congrès armait nécessairement contre lui la population canadienne et violait lui-même ces règles de justice éternelle sur lesquelles il voulait asseoir sa déclaration des droits de l'homme."

Pp. 368, 369, 370. "Les commissaires arrivèrent à Montréal le 29 avril, 1776; Franklin en repartit le 11 mai, peu de jours après la levée du siège de Québec; le P. Carroll le suivit le lendemain. Franklin n'avait pas été longtemps en Canada sans voir que tous ses efforts seraient inutiles: les Canadiens se rappelaient avec quelle ardeur il avait engagé l'Angleterre à entreprendre la conquête de leur pays, vingt ans auparavant. Le Congrès fit donc une faute en l'envoyant vers eux, puisque son nom devait plutôt réveiller dans les coeurs des souvenirs d'hostilité et de vengeance que des sentiments de sympathic et d'union. . . . . Pendant que Franklin s'adressait au peuple canadien, le P (ère) Carroll, en sa qualité d'ecclésiastique, visitait une partie des membres du clergé de Montréal et des campagnes. Il eut encore moins de succès que Franklin. Vainement voulut-il employer les raisons que pouvaient avoir quelque poids dans leur esprit; ils surent en trouver d'autres pour y répondre. Ils lui firent observer que le Grande-Bretagne remplissait les stipulations des traités, que le gouvernement couvrait maintenant de sa protection les anciennes lois et coutumes. . . . On rappela à Carroll que la religion catholique n'avait encore jamais été admise dans telles et telles provinces; que les prêtres en étaient exclus sous des peines très sévères, et que les missionaires envoyés chez leurs sauvages étaient traités avec rigueur et cruauté. On n'était pas persuadé que toutes ces vexations fussent l'œuvre exclusive du gouvernement royal,

Benjamin Franklin's Mission to Canada.

d'autant que, quand il s'agissait des catholiques, les colons américains n'étaient jamais bien prompts à faire respecter le droit sacré de la conscience. Enfin, il y avait de singulières contradictions entre l'adresse du Congrès au peuple de l'Angleterre (du 21 octobre, 1774) et celle au peuple du Canada (du 26 octobre). . . . Cette contradiction entre les deux adresses avait porté ses fruits. Quand on lut dans une réunion de royalistes, la partie de la première relative à la réorganisation du Canada, avec la peinture qu'on y faisait de la religion et des usages de ses habitants, l'assemblée exprima sou ressentiment par des exclamations pleines de mépris. 'O le traître et perfide Congrès. . . . Benissons notre bon prince; restons fidèles à un roi dont l'humanité s'étend à toutes les religions: abhorrons ceux qui veulent nos faire manquer au loyalisme, et dont les promesses sout mensongères.'

Ainsi les propositions pompeuses du Congrès finissaient par n'être plus écoutés. Et le clergé et les seigneurs reprenaient leur ascendant sur le peuple. . . ."

Andrew Bell: *History of Canada, Montreal*, 1862. This is a translation of an earlier edition of Garneau, Vol. 2, pp. 146–149. Practically the same as quoted from Garneau.

William Kingsford: *The History of Canada.* Toronto and London, 1893, Vol. 6, pp. 65–70: details the fact but gives no opinion as to the causes of the failure.

Frank Basil Tracy: *The Tercentenary History of Canada*, N. Y. and Toronto, 1908, Vol. 2, pp. 598, 599. "The Commissioners . . . were accompanied by a brother of Charles Carroll. . . a Jesuit. . . . The object of his participation in the expedition was undoubtedly that of influencing the habitants on their religious side. This cannot be said to be the most worthy way of bringing about the result desired; but as their case was rather desperate at that time, the Americans evidently were willing to adopt extreme means to accomplish their ends. The commissioners used all arguments possible. They even tentatively suggested that Canada might be allowed to retain an independent position in its relation to the rest of the States. They were received very cordially by the people of Montreal and in general . . . wherever they went, but the mission was a complete failure. . . ."

W. H. P. Clement: *The History of the Dominion of Canada*, Toronto, 1897, p. 113, simply notes the facts and that the "mission was a failure."

Sir S. P. Lucas: *A History of Canada, 1763–1812*, Oxford, 1909, p. 122. "The commissioners were three in number. One was Benjamin Franklin, and another was Carroll who was accompanied by his brother, a Jesuit priest. The object was to ascertain the actual position of matters military and political and to conciliate Canadian feeling. What was ascertained was depressing enough and the efforts at conciliation came to nothing."

Rev. William H. Withrow. D.D.: *A Popular History of the Dominion of Canada*, Toronto, 1884, p. 281, much the same as Lucas.

Charles Roger: *The Rise of Canada from Barbarism to Wealth and Civilization*, Quebec, 1856, Vol. 1 (all ever published) p. 62.

Benjamin Franklin's Mission to Canada.

"The American Congress appointed Dr. Benjamin Franklin, Samuel Chase and Charles Carroll of Carrollton—the last mentioned gentleman being requested to prevail upon his brother, the Revd. John Carroll, a Jesuit of distinguished theological attainments and celebrated for his amiable manners and polished address to accompany them—to proceed to Canada. . . . They (the Canadians) were to have the power of self-government, while a free press was to be established to reform all abuses. The . . . Commission were . . . far from being successful in their attempt to negotiate Canada into revolt. The clergy of Canada could not be persuaded that as Roman Catholics they would be better treated by the Revolutionary colonists than they had been under the British government after the expression of such sentiments as those addressed to the people of Great Britain, on the 21st of October, 1774. The Americans, uncouth in manners were, in truth, most intolerant of papacy."

Most of the Canadian Histories, e.g., Bibaud, McMullen, Bryce, &c., say nothing of this missison. American Histories are readily accessible and I extract the references from a few only.

Of two American works specially concerning the attempt to bring Canada in line with the Thirteen Colonies, one, Charles Henry Jones: *History of the Campaign for the Conquest of Canada in 1776*, Philadelphia, 1882, pp. 33, 34, says little of the commission. John Carroll failed, "for the clergy were unanimous against the American cause"—a clear mistake.

The other, Justin H. Smith, *Our Struggle for the Fourteenth Colony*, N. Y. and London, 1907, gives a very full account.

Vol. 2, pp. 325–343; 350–352; 354–356.

"John Carroll . . . met a wall of adamant," p. 334, sums up that part of the story.

In Kate Mason Rowland's *The Life of Charles Carroll*, N. Y. and London, 1898, Vol. 1, pp. 140–176 is an account of the Canadian Commission and its failure—the author says:

Pp. 146, 147. "Unfortunately, indiscreet politico-religious utterances of Congress had offended the French Canadians and rendered them distrustful of their new friends, while the exactions of the Continental soldiery, who with an insufficient commissariat and no money were forced to forage on the natives for subsistence, widened the breach. In truth Canada . . . had by the Quebec Bill of 1774 been given all that she could desire in the way of civil and religions liberty . . . and the Quebec Bill . . . was one of their (i.e. the Americans') acts of indictment against the English Crown."

The Canada Journal of Charles Carroll printed in an appendix to this volume from the Maryland Historical Society's *Centennial Memorial*, speaks under date, May 11, 1776, of "the bad prospect of our affairs in Canada" but gives no reasons—there is no entry from April 29 until May 11, the period of Franklin's stay.

In John Bigelow's *The Life of Benjamin Franklin*, London, 1879, Vol. 2, pp. 354–359 are given Franklin's letters when he was Commissioner

Benjamin Franklin's Mission to Canada.

to Canada. P. 358, May 27, Walker and his wife overtook Franklin "at Saratoga where they both took such liberties in taunting us at our conduct in Canada, that it almost came to a quarrel."

In the same letter (to the Commissioners in Canada from New York, May 27, 1776) Franklin says: "I find I grow daily more feeble and think I could hardly have got along so far but for Mr. Carroll's friendly assistance and tender care of me. Some symptoms of the gout now appear, which makes me think my indisposition has been a smothered fit of that disorder. . . ." To which the editor rather unkindly adds the note, p. 359, "The Doctor's health was always a convenient excuse when he did not wish to give a better. It is not, likely, however, that he would have returned so abruptly if he had not found a state of feeling on the border which was fatal to any co-operation of the Canadians with the revolting colonies."